797,885 Books
are available to read at

www.ForgottenBooks.com

Forgotten Books' App
Available for mobile, tablet & eReader

ISBN 978-1-330-50194-8
PIBN 10070520

This book is a reproduction of an important historical work. Forgotten Books uses state-of-the-art technology to digitally reconstruct the work, preserving the original format whilst repairing imperfections present in the aged copy. In rare cases, an imperfection in the original, such as a blemish or missing page, may be replicated in our edition. We do, however, repair the vast majority of imperfections successfully; any imperfections that remain are intentionally left to preserve the state of such historical works.

Forgotten Books is a registered trademark of FB &c Ltd.
Copyright © 2017 FB &c Ltd.
FB &c Ltd, Dalton House, 60 Windsor Avenue, London, SW19 2RR.
Company number 08720141. Registered in England and Wales.

For support please visit www.forgottenbooks.com

1 MONTH OF FREE READING

at

www.ForgottenBooks.com

By purchasing this book you are eligible for one month membership to ForgottenBooks.com, giving you unlimited access to our entire collection of over 700,000 titles via our web site and mobile apps.

To claim your free month visit:

www.forgottenbooks.com/free70520

* Offer is valid for 45 days from date of purchase. Terms and conditions apply.

English
Français
Deutsche
Italiano
Español
Português

www.forgottenbooks.com

Mythology Photography **Fiction**
Fishing Christianity **Art** Cooking
Essays Buddhism Freemasonry
Medicine **Biology** Music **Ancient Egypt** Evolution Carpentry Physics
Dance Geology **Mathematics** Fitness
Shakespeare **Folklore** Yoga Marketing
Confidence Immortality Biographies
Poetry **Psychology** Witchcraft
Electronics Chemistry History **Law**
Accounting **Philosophy** Anthropology
Alchemy Drama Quantum Mechanics
Atheism Sexual Health **Ancient History**
Entrepreneurship Languages Sport
Paleontology Needlework Islam
Metaphysics Investment Archaeology
Parenting Statistics Criminology
Motivational

SERMONS

BY THE LATE
JOHN SERVICE, D.D.
MINISTER OF HYNDLAND ESTABLISHED CHURCH, GLASGOW

*WITH PREFATORY NOTICE
AND PORTRAIT*

London
MACMILLAN AND CO.
1884

All rights reserved

CONTENTS.

	PAGE
PREFATORY NOTICE,	vii
I.—A HIGHWAY IN THE WILDERNESS,	1
II.—DIVINE DISCONTENT: A COMMUNION SERMON,	27
III.—THE CARCASE AND THE EAGLES,	48
IV.—METHODS OF SPIRITUAL TREATMENT,	73
V.—TRYING TO DO ONE'S BEST,	92
VI.—THE RIGHT OF THE POOR,	114
VII.—CONSIDER THE LILIES,	136
VIII.—TO WHOM IT SHALL BE GIVEN,	159
IX.—PRESENT OPPORTUNITIES,	179
X.—A MULTITUDE OF THE HEAVENLY HOST,	195
XI.—THE LAST JUDGMENT,	216
XII.—THE VALLEY OF THE SHADOW OF DEATH,	243

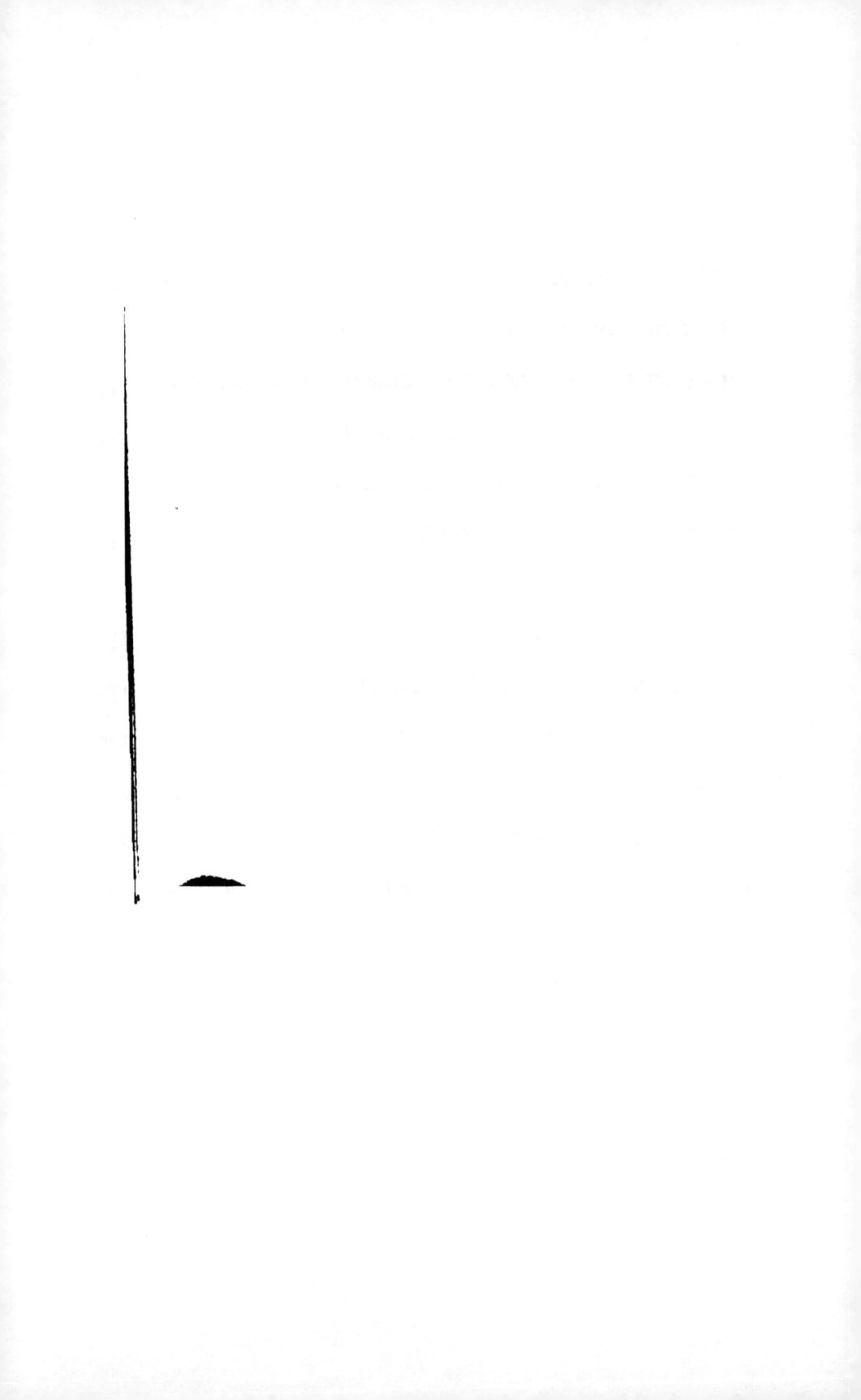

PREFATORY NOTICE.

JOHN SERVICE was born on February 26, 1833, at Campsie, a village within ten miles of the Clyde, at the foot of the Campsie Hills, the range which first swells upward from the Western Lowlands of Scotland towards the Western Highlands guarding Loch Lomond and Loch Katrine. His father was employed as an engraver in the print-works of Mr. Robert Dalglish, for many years M.P. for Glasgow. The boy received the rudiments of his education in the parish school from a master whom he described as a good teacher but rather a severe disciplinarian. It is remembered of his school days that he once wrote an essay which was considered to be so obviously beyond what a boy of his age could possibly produce that his master thrashed him soundly for it. While still very young he entered the print-works as a clerk, and it was his custom between four and five in the morning to go down to the gatehouse of the works, where there were fire and light, to have an hour's quiet reading before the day's task began. Throughout Mr. Dalglish's life, the boy owed a great deal to the interest his employer had soon learned to take in him—an interest which developed afterwards into a warm friendship. At fifteen, Service entered the University of Glasgow, to study for the Church with a view to the ministry. "We recall him," says one of his earliest college friends, Professor Nichol, of Glasgow, "as one of the brightest of our college contemporaries, marked even then, as through life, by much of that apparent inertia which is the frequent accompaniment of some forms of genius; but already, in occasional essays, at social meetings, in rural walks, exhibiting that quiet and lasting quality as distinct from the restless activity of 'all the talents'; throwing out jets of a humour which delighted the discriminating and was a terror to the foolish." He took no very prominent place in college classes, for he was careless of academic honours, and, like many Scotch students, he had to do something to earn his bread during his student days. For several years most of his time was occupied in literary work. He edited the *Dumbarton Herald* for a few months in 1857, and in the following year, and till 1862, he was sub-editor, under Mr. P. E. Dove, of "Mackenzie's Imperial Dictionary of Universal Biography"—

a work which was produced in consecutive parts during several years in Glasgow, and which served students of literary and intellectual promise as a sort of exercise ground, and provided some of them with an introduction to well-known literary men connected with it as contributors. It was probably in this way that Service came under the influence of Professor J. P. Nichol, the author of the "Architecture of the Heavens," and to that distinguished man, who inspired all who were so fortunate as to know him personally with some spark of his own philosophic, philanthropic, and religious enthusiasm, he owed what was probably the most powerful intellectual and moral impulse of his youth. His literary work, and probably some of the scruples arising from the too rigid interpretation that was then commoner than now of the most systematic of Church standards, that often entangled the feet of the best aspirants to the ministry, delayed his entrance into the Church, which took place, however, in 1862. Three years previously, in 1859, he had been married, at Glasgow, to Jessie, second daughter of Mr. James Bayne, teacher of music there. His first ministerial work was in Hamilton, near Glasgow, where he acted for ten months as substitute for Mr. Robertson, then minister of the second parochial charge. After this brief apprenticeship in Hamilton, where—as in every place in which he subsequently lived—he made friends to whom his death last March came as a personal calamity, his health gave way, and he was advised to go to Australia. During the voyage he suffered terribly from the heat of the tropics. On his arrival, the doctors advised him, for the sake of the advantages of riding and driving, to go up country about 150 miles to a place called Wedderburn. What a picture he gives us in *Novantia* of the Australian bush:—" Much of it, as everybody knows, is a treeless plain; more is flat champaign with trees of great size, immense height, and ridiculously scanty foliage, scattered over it as oaks and elms and beeches are scattered for show over an English park. Denude its trees of all their lower branches and three-fourths of their upper ones, and all but a sorry remnant of their foliage (to fly like a remainder of a tattered flag), then shoot them up into the air to twice or three times their natural height, then flood the sky above them and the earth beneath them with the light of an Italian instead of an English sun, widen prodigiously the horizon, remove the east a long way farther from the west, and let the firmament be immensely lifted up as well as illuminated, then scatter clumps and patches of glossy evergreen shrubs among the trees, and your English park will be not a bad imitation of the Australian bush.

Lucus a non lucendo is the frequent reflection of travellers in Australia who have had the advantage in their youth of classical training, of whom there are not a few to be met with, long strangers to classical pursuits—'bush here,' says such a traveller to himself, because for the next fifty miles there is not a shrub to shelter a lizard from the stinging ray, and because the next hundred are as open as Greenwich Park."

The climate in Wedderburn, however, proved several degrees hotter than in Melbourne itself, and suited him still worse, so that he was obliged to return to Melbourne for his own health as well as for that of his infant daughter, who died there. He remained in Australia about eighteen months, and he was about to return to Scotland, when he was advised to make a trial of Hobart Town, in Tasmania, where a Presbyterian minister was required. He went there in January, 1866, and was inducted to St. John's Presbyterian Church in May. After three years his health greatly improved and he thought of returning home, but his friends persuaded him to stay a year longer. No doubt there was much that was interesting and curious in the records of Van Dieman's Land, as Tasmania used to be called, and, with his vivid sense of the humours and contrasts of life he could not fail to be interested in a colony that had begun its career as a nation of criminals—"a peculiar people," as his own David Groats expresses it in *Novantia*, "chosen for breach of the Ten Commandments." "At the time of his residence here," says the most intimate of his Hobart Town friends, "the Presbyterian Church in Tasmania was almost wrecked by internal dissensions, which were a constant source of pain to him, while his congregation was small and by no means rich. Yet with all these disadvantages, and in spite of the small interest that people here take in theological matters, he had succeeded in winning his way to a very general appreciation, and his departure called forth a strong feeling of regret. It was only afterwards that one could measure the remarkable influence he had exerted during his short stay here, an influence by no means limited to those of his own church. The good results can still be traced in many directions in a broader and healthier spirit in Christian work and teaching. For myself," writes Mr. Walker, "I mourn him as a friend who was without an equal, as one to whom I owe more, I think, than any man; and there are many in Hobart Town besides myself who, in spite of the long lapse of years, have watched his career in the old country with eager interest, and who now cherish his memory with the warmest affection." How much Service saw and learned in the island Paradise of Tasmania, rendered all brilliant and ethereal by the most bewitching of climates, among these descendants of pilgrim fathers who had left their native country under compulsion, in the days when transportation to Van Dieman's Land and Botany Bay were favourite rewards for all offences down to sheep stealing, one may read in *Novantia,* and in the papers on Convicts and Quakers, afterwards published in *Good Words.*

He returned to Glasgow in May, 1870. For a year afterwards he was without ministerial duty, but in 1871 he became assistant to the Rev. Charles Strong—then in Anderston, and lately minister of the Scots Church, Melbourne—one of whose earliest duties on his return to this country was to preach the funeral sermon of his friend and former colleague. "Back in Scotland," says Professor Nichol speaking of this period, "and adrift on the sea of letters he wrote some of the most careful and incisive reviews" and articles "that have appeared in the columns of the (*Glasgow*) *Herald,* but he was too severe a thinker to have a ready pen, and could only write when the spirit moved. Nor, in preaching on trial, would he condescend to humour his congregations by breadth of platitude, exalted by strength of lung. Mr. Service was in danger of submersion; when, in the latter days of patronage, the Earl of Stair detected his worth, and appointed him to the charge of the parish of Inch. There he remained for several years a retired student, enriching his already well-laden mind with the classics of England and Germany; a model pastor, endearing himself to his flock, like George Herbert, by numberless acts of kindliness; by virtue of his perfect courtesy and independence, at his ease in castle and cottage alike, associating with friends from whose minds the remembrance of rambles and drives, made vivid by flashes of pathos and wit that never failed, will never fade. This period gave birth to his two most considerable works, the romance of *Novantia* (in *Good Words*), which afterwards appeared (1875) under the title of *Lady Hetty*, and a volume of sermons. A medley of the author's experience in Hobart Town and by the shores of Loch Ryan, its graphic sketches, wise saws, and dramatic situations, afford matter to stock a dozen ordinary novels; but some mismanagement in the plot restricted the range of its appreciative admirers, though it was translated and received with approval by our more analytical neighbours abroad. The volume entitled *Salvation Here and Hereafter* attained a wider popularity, and carried the name of the author over the borders to England, where the book was welcomed and esteemed. It is on the whole the most remarkable published record of the Scottish pulpit that has appeared during the last quarter of a century. Allured by a cordial invitation, and induced by consideration for the welfare of his family, whom he had himself been educating in the old manse on the isolated lake peninsula, Dr. Service, who had about this time accepted the degree of D.D. from his University, re-migrated to Glasgow as minister of the West-end church of Hyndlands, in the discharge of the duties of which he remained till his death."

"His life in Inch," writes one who was intimately acquainted with his habits, "was very quiet. His health was pretty good. His practice was to write his sermons in the morning, and in the afternoon he either drove or walked into Stranraer, the little country town three miles off, spent an hour or two with a couple of intimate friends and returned home between four and five o'clock." Few of his brother clergymen, perhaps, were in sympathy with his views, but he was as much a favourite with them as with his people. He never seemed to tire of his manse, known as Soulseat, in memory of the old abbey, the site of which it occupied, where generations of the monks, whose bones lay thick about, had lived their long-forgotten lives. The old churchyard—a few stones of the old church—the manse or minister's residence, and a pleasant field or two of orchard and garden hung together and alone on the little lake-washed peninsula. Here, after his world-wide wanderings, the minister of Inch might well have let himself be rocked to sleep by the winds of the North Channel sweeping through his firs and yew trees, and the plash of the waters of his lake on the reeds and pebbles of its shores. His first impressions of the place may be given in his own words:—"Novantia was in its later glory (it had one of spring and one of summer, the one more splendid, the other more rich and various) when its new owner came into possession. To him it was a dream—an island, not in water, but in the skies. Exquisite as a picture even to a common eye, to him it was rich in that beauty of association and memory which is the soul of other and more material loveliness. The orchard, with its patriarchal trees, barren now, and overgrown with moss and lichen even to the tips of their tiniest and loftiest twigs, sloped to the rising sun. Here, beyond doubt, did the holy monks walk and talk after early matins in the days of old. By holy hands these trees were planted. Their barrenness to the sense was a harvest to the soul: their grey mosses and lichens were to the imagination apples of gold in pictures of silver. As for the garden, it sloped with a distinctly utilitarian view towards the south; but it had been cultivated doubtless by other than mechanic hands, and with other than sordid thoughts, for ages and ages. To the north and west the foot-path which followed the curvings of the loch wound through elms and beeches of large size, a long leafy cloister. Here no doubt was the evening walk of the prior and his clergy, when the sun, then as now, was going down in front, and pouring across the dull expanse of water a broad river of gold." But his Inch life was fruitful of work. Dr. Service is nowhere better or stronger than in *Novantia*, and his deepest convictions are never more clearly or forcibly expressed than in the pregnant words of David Groats, the gatekeeper, a reminiscence of those starlit winter mornings when the bright-eyed little lad sat at the feet of the Gamaliel of the print work.

It was chiefly, perhaps, for the sake of the education of his family, but it was partly, no doubt, due to the promptings of lifelong friendships with men like his college contemporaries, Professors Nichol and Edward Caird, who were settled as teachers in his old University, and of other intimate friends like Principal Caird, the Rev. Dr. Brown of Paisley, and Mr. Douglas Dykes of Hamilton, that he was induced to accept the call of the newly-formed congregation of Hyndlands Church to be their first minister. Certainly the motive that counted least with him was any kind of ambition, though the intellectual horizon of Glasgow was likely, in some respects at least, to be wider than that of Inch. In his country parish he left behind him friends to whom familiar intercourse with his bright and tender nature had come to be counted as perhaps the richest blessing of their lives :—

"Dr. Service's goodness and kindness," writes one from his old parish of Inch, who loved and venerated him, "have been inexpressible, and in more than one great sorrow he has been to us more than our nearest kin. It seems hard as yet to realize that he will come no more among us, brightening our dwelling as no other friend ever did. Our friend was so little of the ecclesiastic and so much the father of his people. By his geniality, frankness, and universal kindness to all, especially the suffering and poor, irrespective of denomination, he had endeared himself to everybody before he had almost time to settle in his new parish."

The Sermons in this volume may be taken to indicate the nature and character of his teaching in Glasgow. The impression he made there is faithfully represented in the words of his life-long friends, Professor Nichol and Professor Edward Caird, written under the first shock of unexpected loss. Professor Nichol says :—

"Death has taken perhaps the finest and most original,

certainly the most dauntless, religious teacher of the West of Scotland, in whom the Church will miss a unique type —that of a man who knew the world well, and yet was not of it, who, saturated with the spirit of Christ, has been for half his comparatively brief life preaching a new, or rather reviving an old, Christianity. Under the shadow we can only speak of him in stammering words. The mists of fresh bereavement must be allowed to lift themselves slowly from our memories of the most genial and yet the truest of friends. . . . The custom of judging a man from the impression left by his personality and work during the later years of his life is in the case of Dr. Service more than usually fair; for in them were gathered up the results of his varied experience, the mellow harvests of his thought. The edge of his intellect was never dulled by lassitude; the sword of his righteous warfare grew sharper by use; the grasp of his almost apostolic love became more comprehensive and more close. The comparatively few intimate friends of a man whose modesty and physical weakness prevented the circle from being greatly enlarged, can alone appreciate the loss of his social charm. To them the absence of the winning smile, the cordial grasp, the congratulation in good fortune, the almost personal share his nature constrained him to take in every crisis of sickness or sorrow, cannot be translated into words. Their testimony to their loss must remain in their inexpressible sense of an irreparable blank in their lives. . . . On the surface of his sermons there played a humour, often as subtle as that of Lamb, often as incisive as that of Sydney Smith—a satire as trenchant as that of Carlyle against every shade of insincerity. Beneath, alongside of the most searching criticism of what is commonly called the supernatural, there was what might be thought an almost supernatural faith in the perfectibility of mankind, and in the sufficiency of a trust in an overruling Providence. He had seen and encountered as much of the worry and weariness and vexation of the world as most of his fellows, but his trust never wavered in the continuous progression of the race towards that assimilation with the divine which he held to be its destiny. Morally he was the most charitable of pureminded men. Not Swift himself spoke with more savage force against quacks and smooth-tongued rogues and the conscious vendors of cowardly compromise. But, as with his Master, his hatred of vice never maimed his compassion for the vicious. He was wont, to the verge of reasonable tolerance, to attribute even their worst errors, not to an evil star, but to ignorance and the unhappy environments of what he regarded as even now only a dimly dawning civilization, a faint promise of that perfect Socialism, towards which, in the faith of his constantly spiritualized Darwinism he held the whole creation moved. This charity of judgment was carried almost to an extreme in his dealing with the vices of the poor. To 'sins of blood' in all ranks he was amply tolerant, while his indignation was roused as much against deliberate traduction or inveterate malignity as against consistent selfishness or triumphant fraud."

Professor Caird says:—

"Glasgow has lost one of those influences that work with little noise or outward show. To the larger public he was comparatively little known, but no one who came in contact with him failed to carry away an impression of that clear and marked individuality which stamps itself on the mind like a living force, in contrast with the blurred images of ordinary acquaintanceship. His simple manliness, his unaffected cordiality of soul, his fellow-feeling for the poor, the oppressed, and even for the morally diseased, his ever-fresh interest in all the things of the intellect and the spirit, his freedom from every shade of superstition, his intolerance of pretence and obscurantism, rescued as it was from any suspicion of bitterness by the kindly touch of a humorous sympathy that held nothing human alien—when shall we see these things again, and how shall they who have seen ever forget them?

Humour, indeed, is one of the first words that come to our lips when we speak of Dr. Service. His was a humour that, mingling with all his words and actions, could not be kept out—if he ever thought to keep it out —of his sermons. But in his hand it did not seem incongruous there; for it was a humour springing from that keen sense of the littleness of things great and the greatness of things little in human life, which it is a mark of a great teacher to realize. Unassuming, even unceremonious in bearing, he produced, nevertheless, an impression of inner refinement, of magnanimity, and purity of mind, which only grew with growing acquaintance. There was, on a superficial view, very little of the cleric about him; he had long emancipated himself from most of the dogmatic forms which seem to many to be identified with Christianity; yet there have been few men more truly filled with the spirit of Christ. His indifference to theology in the technical sense rendered only more striking his direct view of the lessons conveyed, and his spiritual reception of the life recorded, in the Gospels. With this there had grown up in him an intense conviction of the unchristian character of much of the structure of our modern social life—a conviction which was only not socialistic because he did not readily accept any outward nostrum for the cure of our social diseases. He had next to no value for the shows of life; his feelings were for the many rather than for the few; if he could be unjust, it was toward the ecclesiastical politician and the priest who made much of his office. But no one who had even casually attended his church could fail to be impressed with the deep devotional spirit which was expressed, perhaps most conspicuously, in his prayers. And he had, above all, as many can testify, the distinctive gift of a Christian pastor, the healing touch, the gift of consolation, which made him ever welcome in the house of suffering."

We may be permitted to close these reminiscences with the words in which the obituary notice of the *Glasgow Herald* of March 17th expressed the public sense of the loss the city had sustained:—

"When Dr. Service came to Glasgow it was to continue the same teaching in a wider sphere. Liberty and religion were his watchwords, and only his own congregation and those who occasionally heard him preach in the High Church or in the College Chapel, where he drew larger audiences of young men than any one but the Principal, knew how his powers were growing, his nature deepening and broadening, and his teaching becoming at once more independent and more religious. He had learned to look life and death, man and God, in the face, in love and without fear. The passion at his heart, the passion to say or do something to turn the hearts of others to 'consider the poor;' burned clearer and stronger in him every day of his life. His later teaching was essentially the same as that of the Master whom he served. Few preachers of modern times, or indeed of any time, have reminded their hearers as constantly as he did of the sermons that were preached on the hillsides of Palestine two thousand years ago. It was this "Galilean gospel" that he preached continually, with the same burdens and the same refrains, warm with all the love and pity and scorn and passionate indignation of a nature embracing and at the same time understanding all sorts and conditions of men. The central figure to which he always came back was the figure of Christ. The lesson he never tired of urging on his hearers was that "imitation of Christ" which has done so much, and yet, perhaps, considering all that there was to do, so little to transform the world. It was his to see, and few men were as able to make others see the pathos, as well as the comedy of human lives. His humour darted and glowed round and among the perpetual subjects of his teaching—man's aims and hopes, his duties and his future, his miseries and his greatness—like the lightning that illumines the darkness of a summer night, and makes plain the essential nature and relationships of things that have become commonplace in the familiar day. Though he never attracted great crowds, there was not, for a cultivated audience, so fascinating a preacher in all Scotland. Standing aside from theological and ecclesiastical controversies, breathing a clearer air, he seemed to see farther and with surer insight into the tendencies of living thought and the religious future of mankind. It is our frequent misfortune in Scotland not to know the treasure we have in such a teacher till he is with us no longer. Should it be found possible for something at least of his later work to be given to the world, we shall certainly recognise the wealth we have missed in the unexhausted possibilities of a life which was growing clearer and stronger and fuller till its unexpected close. His congregation and his personal friends know that their loss is irreparable. Those who speak without reserve all the truth that is in their hearts, who differ widely from prevailing views, and who have constantly to discuss questions touching men's highest hopes and their deepest fears, must count on awakening dislikes and alarms in the minds even of sincere and good men. But, in spite of the startling distinctness with which he always expressed whatever he felt himself constrained to say, there were very few who feared or disliked Dr. Service. It was hardly possible for anybody to misunderstand him—it was impossible for those who knew him even but a little not to love him."

The sermons in this volume have been selected by friends of the author from a considerable number of his manuscripts. Dr. Service wrote out his sermons pretty fully for immediate use in the course of his ordinary ministry, and only very slight changes have been made in preparing them for the press. Here and there a colloquial expression, suitable enough for oral delivery, or an obvious expansion and repetition of the same thought, have been omitted. The selection of sermons has been made with a view, as far as possible, to represent the general character of the author's preaching, especially during the period of his five years' ministry in Glasgow. It is hoped that they will be sufficient to show the wide range of the subjects he brought before his congregation, and to indicate how boldly and yet how reverently he dealt with the questions pressing most urgently on the minds of men in our day. They may serve to recall the mode of thought of one who exercised a unique influence on all those who listened to his preaching, as well as on those with whom he came personally into contact.

The leading ideas of these sermons will be more or less familiar to the numerous readers of the volume entitled "Salvation Here and Hereafter," a volume which, "in the honesty of his heart, he published, in order, I know," says the Rev. Charles Strong, "to make clear to others his position in the Church, leaving it to the Church to declare whether he had gone beyond the bounds of toleration or not." In the present, as in the former volume, it is in the character of Christ that the author finds the highest expression of religion. It is to the life of Christ, the teaching of Christ, the example of Christ, that he constantly recurs. The elaborate theological system in which Christian ideas were crystallized by the greatest of Christ's immediate followers seems never to have laid much hold on Dr. Service's mind. To his thinking, the Master himself seemed to speak with more vivid and persuasive force to the thoughts and feelings of our time than all his expositors. Every religious teacher of any measure of originality sees truth in his own way, and so long as it is truth that he preaches, it is of little consequence though the aspects of it which have special attractions for other minds should in his preaching be kept in abeyance, or altogether ignored. It was the object of Dr. Service's life to distinguish what he believed to be the essentials of Christianity from its accidents and accompaniments, and to show how in these essentials it was in perfect agreement with that other and earlier revelation which is contained in nature and in the individual and social life of man, though it may sometimes be as difficult for us to decipher it as to find the secret of the palimpsest under the trivialities with which it has been covered. It was his chief aim and effort to direct men's thoughts to the foundations on which the edifice of Christian living as well as Christian thinking must be built. In his effort to accomplish this, he appears at times almost an iconoclast, and he may even seem occasionally to speak of many things which others have deemed essential as so much hay and straw and stubble. He spoke as he believed —he spoke it as passionately as he believed it. But it was always his main end and object to ascertain what was real and beyond dispute, in an age in which much that is essential has been challenged or denied. In all life, secular and religious, he recognises a divine order, a central and all-comprehending government of the universe—" What is well done to-day is well done for ever. Being taken up into the life of humanity, its effects not only outlive the individual, but one way and another must survive the race itself, and go out into space wherever God is. If there is anything in the world of a divine presence, of a divine order, this is part of the reality of it." In his view, the main business of the religious teacher to-day must be what it has always been —to reconcile divine order and human disorder—to bring "heaven nearer the centre of London and Glasgow." In the effort he was sustained by the conviction that he was working with the permanent forces of the universe. "The good increases, the evil steadily diminishes. That I believe, as I believe in God. That I take to be Christian belief, if ever any belief was what Christ's was." In this progress of the good he never loses faith. "There is progress, though it be slow and unequal. That, let me say, in conclusion, is the great truth which we have to keep in mind so as not to lose heart in well-doing. It is because, among unnumbered generations of men, countless individuals have lived by the rule of trying to do their best in spite of difficulties and reverses, that we are where we are to-day with our hopes of to-morrow and of heaven." It is because this is so that man forever finds new heart and courage to live as Christ teaches him to live—" To live for others, in the lives of others, a wider, truer, intenser life than that of the selfish mind, is the best of life according to the definition of the good which is to be found in the Gospel of Christ. It is not a commandment given from heaven, with rewards and penalties to give it weight, which makes that the best of life; it is the very nature of things, it is the very make and constitution of human nature." In the light that is thrown on the world by thus living, it is always growing younger, larger, better. "Nothing has been lost, nothing has perished from the world which was ever found in it by those loftier and nobler spirits of our race to whom it has been most glorious and divine. In regard to what concerns the life of the intellect and the life of the soul—that which a man has in himself, and which makes him a conscious being—the world is the same to-day as it has been since man became man, only enriched by age instead of impoverished. Every morning that restores to light what the night concealed, and that recalls the soul to consciousness of itself, makes all things new, as new as they were at the dawn of creation." All men are born into this inheritance of divine beauty. It was his constant and passionate cry that its treasures should be made available to them all, and especially to the poor. "It is, above all, not with reference to the amusement of the idle few, but with reference to the social, moral, religious refinement and advancement of the toiling and degraded many, that the beautiful has its claims to be considered as among the first and foremost of human interests."

It is this spirit aflame with the desire to raise all that is low, to refine all that is degraded, to recover and restore all that is lost, which he recognises in the Christianity of the Saviour of men. In the opportunities that every life is always bringing with it, he found the oil which is needed, and which is able to keep the fire burning. "Apart from the conditions and circumstances and events of actual life among the poor—call for that life to God and man which is salvation, and no wonder if your voice is that of one crying in the wilderness, or, rather, at the corners of the streets, where hundreds of voices drown each other. But in the lives of the poor, in their relations with each other and with those who show them sympathy, in their experience of want and sickness and neglect, and in the response which suffering makes to suffering, deep answering to deep in human life—in all this, human nature on its better and nobler side—that of patience and goodness and love—has that chance of cultivating itself which is the chance of salvation." In the lives of honest and good poor men, unconventional, unconscious, he sees the solid foundations of human society—foundations not less wonderful or divine than those splendours of the mystical city of God which blaze in the Apocalypse. "Reserve your reverence for such an one as you sometimes see returning from his work in the fields, in the factory, in the mine—a son of toil prematurely aged by work, his back bent, his limbs stiffened and distorted—returning from his slavish toil to what would seem to you a wretched, but is to him a cheerful, home of which he is the light and happiness. Say, as you meet him, Well done, good and faithful servant! Stop his work, and what can you do by your charity to replace it? Stop the work of men like him, and how long would your benevolent societies be able to ward off bankruptcy in trying to feed the hungry and to clothe the naked?"

After life, Death—after Death, the Judgment. All religious teachers in turn—none more perhaps than the Christian—have spent much of their best thought and effort on Death and Judgment. Dr. Service is never tired of explaining that in the judgment there is nothing arbitrary. Christ judges by character—"Inasmuch as ye have done it unto the least of these." "It is man's judgment upon man which is embodied in the Christian representation of the final judgment. Therefore it is final. These distinctions which it makes are everlasting, not to be altered or repealed without re-making man and re-making the world. That which, in presence of the Eternal, is decisive as to the well-being or ill-being of man, is humanity or inhumanity. Here and hereafter, it is the same. In that sense spiritual religion has for its last word, as well as its first, peace, goodwill, compassion, sympathy, kindness, humanity." The other world is as this is, under the same laws, part of the same order, the breath of the same God. "We are under no kind of arbitrary government—it is sure that what a man sows he also reaps, that life is not a lottery but an education, that man has no heaven to hope for and no hell to fear except that which is connected with being true or false to the better nature within him."

It is in the intensity with which he feels that the everyday life of every man is not the barren waste of trivialities it seems to most of us in most hours of the unmemorable days when we are trudging across it, and has in it the breath and stir of the infinite, that a true religious teacher finds the fire which inflames men's hearts as with a live coal from off the altar. In his eyes, everything in daily living is seen to be related to the greatest things and the strongest forces in the movement of the world, and every common life is worked into that living garment which the earth-spirit is for ever weaving for the vesture of Divinity. It is the same feeling that gives immortal power and youth to a great poet of humanity like Burns. Dr. Service's introductory notice of him in Ward's "English Poets" reveals in every line the strength of the sympathy with which the critic recognised his own strongest feelings. "Human nature," he says, "in its most ordinary shapes is more poetical than it looks, and exactly at those moments of its consciousness in which it is most truly because most vividly and powerfully and poetically itself, Burns has a voice to give to it. He is not the poet's poet, which Shelley no doubt meant to be, or the philosopher's poet, which Wordsworth, in spite of himself, is. He is the poet of human nature, not half so homely or prosaic as it seems. His genius, in a manner all its own, associates itself with the fortunes, experiences, memorable moments, of human beings whose humanity is their sole patrimony; to whom 'liberty,' and whatever, like liberty, has the power

> 'To raise a man aboon the brute,
> And mak him ken himsel,'

is their portion in life; for whom the great epochs and never-to-be-forgotten phases of existence are those which are occasioned by emotions inseparable from the consciousness of existence." In this "portrait of a giant painted on a thumb-nail," as he used to describe it, we see Burns as he was—so full of that "divine discontent" which gives force to transform the world that he is rightly to be reckoned as one of the greatest revolutionary forces in Scottish life. "Wherever his countrymen go they carry with them as a feature of the national mind an estimate of man as man, of wealth and worth, of rank and work, which bears the stamp of one man's genius. Burns's poems and songs are a programme of social and political reform and progress, or at any rate aspiration,—as radical a programme as could well be framed. No such programme, it is certain, ever had such currency in one nation as it has obtained among the Scottish race at home and abroad. For almost a century it has been said and sung by high and low, by rank and fashion, by artizans and milkmaids, and aged inmates of the poorhouse. Children babble it and lisp it; it is the privileged sedition of public houses and public assemblies, privileged almost like the Bible; young ladies warble it at the request of their Tory grandfathers and to please their orthodox aunts; in kirks, as well as where the shepherd tells his tale, the echoes of it are never still."

It is the terror of something after death under unknown and awful conditions that, to many, gives death its sharpest sting. But if man is to be judged by his Maker, as the heart that his Maker has given him judges of good and bad here, this life is but the ante-room of the next, and death a flimsy partition. Dr. Service did not think the end of life the important thing—a good death the highest of aims and for a friend the best of wishes. "It cannot be considered the end and aim of existence when the time comes for us to die, to do so with dignity. The larger part of life, if it is to be counted life at all, and not distinguished from death or simply worse than death, must be something in the way of activity, enterprise, enjoyment, rather than mere endurance, however stubborn or heroic." "Heaven there is none for the human soul— hell there is none for it but in itself. The universe is the good man's friend and the bad man's enemy. It is as natural to die as to be born, and all the valley of the shadow of death, except what we make terrible for ourselves by our misdeeds, is an illusion of the mind which clings rather to the shadows of life than to the great reality to which existence is more than life." The sermon with which this volume closes—one of the last and finest which he preached—is full of this teaching. Perhaps the sum and tendency of it is seen as clearly as anywhere at the bedside of David Groats in *Novantia*, when that aged and worn-out saint after Dr. Service's heart is taking his farewell of life. "' I was telling him last night as he sat there a thing I ance saw in your country. It was a fine harvest afternoon, the sun glancing on the stubble fields and the air above as still as the earth below. I was standin' outside the gate, thinkin', maybe, o' some auld story or ither o' my ain, when the rattle o' a cart in the field across the road made me start and look ower the hedge. The farmer was takin' hame his last load, and had jist lifted his last bundle. But he had something yet tae dae. He marched straight ower tae his bogle up on the knowe, lifted him up, and tossed him intae his cart on the top o' his barley. That bogle had been standin' there since the spring time. Many a time I took aff my bonnet and said "Good mornin'" tae him, he imitated humanity so abominably. He had been standin' there, I say, and wi' his villainous auld hat, and his arm stretched out, terrified the craws for near a year. But his time was come—his days were numbered. My frien' the farmer, no lookin' ower his shouther, or kennin' onybody was lookin' at him, or thinkin' there was onything particular in liftin' a bogle mair nor a bundle o' barley, but jist finishin' his harvest the reg'lar way, he hoists him up, and tosses him intae his cart.'

"Hetty was thinking what kind of conversation between the old man and his nephew might have called forth this reminiscence of her native county, and waited to hear his own account of it.

"'Ane meets many bogles in his time,' he said, after

pausing to recover his breath, 'and if he lives as long as I've done, sees many o' them ta'en hame.'

"'And maybe,' said the dominie, who had slipped in before the conclusion of the story, and was now peeping round the curtain at the foot of the bed—'and maybe the Deil himself is a kind of bogle.'

"'To be picked up,' said Hetty, 'at the great harvest.'"

Like the prophet whom perhaps of all his contemporaries he most loved and honoured, Dr. Service, was constantly thinking of what may be after death, as part of that one kingdom of God which, visible to us on this side of our graves, is as real as it is invisible on the other. He would have found no truer expression of his own abiding mind than the words of Thomas Carlyle, a year after the heart seemed to have been crushed out of him by his wife's death.

"Eternity, which cannot be far off, is my one strong city. I look into it fixedly now and then. All terrors about it seem to me superfluous; all knowledge about it, any the least glimmer of certain knowledge, impossible to living mortal. The universe is full of love, but also of inexorable sternness and severity, and it remains for ever true that God reigns. Patience! Silence! Hope!"

A HIGHWAY IN THE WILDERNESS.

"The voice of him that crieth in the wilderness, Prepare ye the way of the Lord, make straight in the desert a highway for our God."—Isaiah xl. 3.

ONE curious result of the revision of the Old Testament, which is now in progress and which will be given to the world it is to be hoped before long, will be this, that passages in the New Testament quoted from the Old Testament, which agree with the originals as given in the present version, will in some instances be found to differ from them. As we all know, this passage at the commencement of the second Book of Isaiah is quoted at the beginning of Matthew's Gospel as applicable to John Baptist. "For this is he that was spoken of by Isaiah the Prophet, saying, The voice of one crying in the wilderness, Make ye ready the way of the Lord, Make his paths straight." I take this from the Revised Version of the New Testament, which of course is as accurate a representation of the original

Greek of the New Testament as you could have. What a remarkable instance of the fulfilment of prophecy! has been the natural reflection of readers of the New Testament from the time there was a New Testament in existence, as it was the reflection of the author of this gospel, whoever he was. How marvellous that Isaiah, eight centuries or so before the time, should have seen John Baptist in the wilderness and heard him cry, "Prepare ye the way of the Lord!"

When we get the new version of the Old Testament, however, in all probability it will appear that there is a difference between the Hebrew of the Old and the Greek of the New Testament which is not represented in our two versions. It is as certain at any rate as anything can well be in regard to the translation of the Old Testament Hebrew into our tongue, that we ought to read here, not "the voice of one crying in the wilderness, Prepare ye the way of the Lord," but rather, "the voice of one crying, Prepare ye in the wilderness the way of the Lord." It is not worth while always to be so very critical about texts. Here perhaps it is excusable. We have heard a good deal of the Septuagint—the translation of the Old Testament into Greek by the Seventy of that city, Alexandria, which was once famous for a library, and which we have made famous again by a bombardment. The writers of the New Testament often use the Septuagint or Greek version of the Old Testament instead of translating from the Hebrew, and that is apparently what has been done in the present instance. In any case, as any one looking at the passage would suspect if his mind were not biassed by another translation being familiar to him, what we ought to read here is what the most exact and reliable modern scholarship proposes to read—not "the voice of one crying in the wilderness," but " the voice of one crying, Prepare ye in the wilderness the way of the Lord." This translation makes a consistent and intelligible unity of the passage—" the voice of one crying, Prepare ye in the wilderness the way of the Lord ; make straight in the desert a highway for our God." Poets and prophets, especially of the Hebrews, love alliteration, repetition, cumulative effect of pictures seen in various lights. Here we have an instance in the words, "Prepare a highway in the wilderness; make ready a path in the desert."

"Never prophecy until you know" is a satirical utterance. But this, at all events, is a good rule—" Never point to fulfilment of prophecy in the sense of prediction until you are sure." It is true no doubt that John Baptist did prepare the way of the Lord, as all the great and good of all times and all lands have helped to prepare it. It is true, perhaps, also that he went out into the wilderness to preach and that people went out there to hear him, though why he did so is not clear; so that in the way of loosely accommodating the Old to the New, which is the habit of the New Testament writers, they were right in saying that here the prophecy of Isaiah was fulfilled. But it is another thing for us to prove by an instance of this kind the truth of a view of prophecy which makes it in the main identical with soothsaying. Except one or two fragments of the prophetic writings which have been taken and applied to Christ himself, with regard to which it has been said that they were fulfilled to the letter in his life, there is not perhaps a bit of prophecy in the Bible on which more stress has been laid than on this supposed prediction of John preaching in the wilderness by Isaiah. Yet one has only to rub his eyes and then open them again to see that prophecy here, as elsewhere, is not prediction at all. Isaiah the Prophet, hundreds of years before the time, foresaw John Baptist preaching in the wilderness; therefore prophecy is prediction, and prediction is a miracle, and a miracle is evidence of I know not what. This is the argument that we are familiar with. But it all turns upon the question of prediction, specific prediction of John Baptist's preaching in the wilderness of Judea. Now "the voice of one crying in the wilderness"—if you read so—will have a sufficiently direct application to John Baptist and to few men besides. But "the voice of one crying, Prepare a highway in the wilderness," is no more exclusively applicable to him than to John Calvin or John Knox or John Ruskin. It is applicable to everybody, who does anything for the world, especially in its waste places and its worst places, in the way of improvement. It is applicable to Copernicus, Bacon, James Watt. Above all it is applicable to Christ himself. If it has a special application to any one, it is to Him and not to His forerunner. We ought now, all of us, young and old, to have another notion of prophecy altogether than that it is first cousin to soothsaying. There are prophets of the Gentiles as well as of the Jews. I need not have said so much on this point, if it were not that so much of our religion is a matter of texts, and therefore not of that kind, of which it may be said, "Not one jot or one tittle of it shall pass away," but of which it may rather be thought, that the living part of it has enough to do to carry the weight of what is dead.

Some time ago, I pointed out at some length the difference between our civilization and the more ancient civilizations, which we know best about, the

Greek for example, and the Roman, in respect of inherent stability. They depended upon, or were inextricably mixed up with, the supremacy of a select class, relatively insignificant, the members of which enjoyed, at the expense of the rest of the community, superabundant advantages for refinement and culture. In its very nature, the position of that class was unstable, and when it was upset, these civilizations were upset along with it. Our civilization rests upon a different footing, upon that of discoveries and inventions by which the necessaries and comforts of life are multiplied and cheapened, and by which the lives of the many are improved and elevated. These discoveries and inventions cannot be lost. For that reason civilization, as we know it, cannot be overthrown or arrested. Retrogression in the matter is inconceivable. Nothing but progress can be imagined or predicted. The fate of religion being involved in the fate of civilization, prophecy with us, when it is prophecy at all, when it is the voice of the Highest of all crying in the speech and in the writings of the highest and best of our time, is not, and needs not be, a dismal croak as to the world being a wilderness. Like this prophecy of an old Hebrew poet and sage, it is an anticipation of better and still better times for all mankind, of the wilderness being reclaimed and beginning to blossom.

Suppose it to be granted, however, that all that can be said in this way by the most sanguine and enthusiastic minds is certain to turn out correct, the question may still be, with some of us, Does it matter so very much, or does it matter at all to us who can have no hope of seeing it in our time, who have certainly, as it would seem, to live out our lives in a condition of things in which not so much the presence of improvement as the need of it is conspicuous? This question is sure to be asked; that it is a question that ought to be asked, may be felt by many who would not venture to ask it in so many words.

To this question, I think, there are two answers, both of which, for religious minds, at any rate, have some weight. One is this: our idea of God, of a divine order in the world, is very much, to use a homely phrase, our whole or nearly our whole stock-in-trade, our means of living, our resource against bankruptcy, destitution, beggary, in the matter of religion. The question with us, as regards religion, is, how much we can see of God in what is not God; and in what seems opposed to God? Is that which we see of Him, though it must be little, yet enough to give us feeling, emotion, the crown and flower of all emotion—to fill our minds, not with a thousand scruples, anxieties and alarms about things clean and unclean, but to fill them to overflowing with reverence, wonder, adoration, all that constitutes the mysterious life of a spirit conversing with that unutterable Spirit behind the veil. Or shall this life which we now lead in the flesh begin and end there, slip away from us as from clean and unclean beasts, without our having known or felt so much of the soul of the universe as this—or felt anything at all? This is the question of religion, the great question. Second to this even, though of infinite importance, is the question whether we shall devour widows' houses and for a pretence make long prayers, or meditate upon the Good Samaritan, and go and do likewise. This, I say, is the question of religion. It obviously then concerns very much our idea of God, our experience of Him, what we see or feel of Him, that is to say, our stock-in-trade in the matter of religion, what notion we form and entertain of the future destiny of mankind. We know that the past has not been all that could be wished. Plenty of desert in that backward view—so much, that with regard to the happy Garden we feel that it is distance which lends it its enchantment. Will the future be better, any better, much better? Evidently and unmistakeably, that is a matter which must go to shape our idea of God, of the divine order of the world. This is to look at the whole instead of a small part and form some conclusion or other about the whole. It does matter a good deal to us, therefore, though we are not to live to see it, that, if it is possible or right to entertain it, we should entertain the belief that the endless, practically endless, ages that are yet to come will exhibit the divine order as beneficent and beautiful in a way in which past ages and our own age have had scanty experience of it.

Another answer to the question, What does it matter to us what the future of mankind may be? is obviously this. It is not so much a duty as an instinct for man to live for posterity. A man will often do for posterity what he could scarcely muster resolution or patience to do for himself—for posterity next to himself, for his own children and grandchildren. His satisfaction in doing that is unbidden, natural, instinctive. That satisfaction is not necessarily limited to posterity in the shape of blood-relations or heirs-at-law. We are all of one stock. It is natural, instinctive to have some feeling of that. The more civilization advances, the more feeling of that there is among men of all classes, even including people who differ from each other and dislike each other. Well, with reference to this instinct and this satisfaction, the case is plain as regards the future being other and better than the past or the present. We have all something to do and can do something for posterity—including first of all, of course, blood-relations and all who ought to be remembered in our last will and testament. To be sure, we have the conviction or the hope in doing this, that it is not going to be in vain. This is a great satisfaction of a natural instinct—in religious minds a powerful instinct—and it is a stimulus as well as a satisfaction. It is a great matter in doing our work, whatever it may be—and we have all got some work to do for the world—if we have an idea that the result of it will be felt in an improvement of the world, of human life, of which there shall be no end; it is a great matter if we should be of opinion that it is not going to be lost in the great dismal swamp of irremediable human wretchedness and misery.

It is with reference to all this, it is upon these grounds that I insist so often and so much that, as being blessed with some measure of religious feeling, as I hope we all are, we who belong to Christian churches should have our principal concern not about churches, not about building many, or endowing many, or attracting crowds to them all; not about religious business, but about other things in regard to which other people cannot or will not take that interest which ought to be taken.

It ought to be left to the non-religious—I don't say to the irreligious, but to those who have no strong feeling of religion, being in and for itself the best of life—to do a great deal of church work, so-called religious work. Let them hope to save their souls by that, as they will do whether you let them or not. There are always people enough anxious to save their own souls by saving other people's souls, and convinced that it is a good way to take. As for those who are anxious not about the prosperity of sects, but the progress of religious reason, those possessing an idea of God, or rather possessed by it, let them support and aid churches as far as they can. But it is for them above all to take thought and pains in regard to all that is secular and, alas! profane in human life and human society, so as to have that so altered and improved as to admit of religion entering into common life where it is excluded now. It is for them to do that just as far as they have something of a real belief in the eternal order, and because they can find a reward in doing it, and will have a support and strength in doing it in the feeling that it is certain to be eternally productive. They do save their souls by this method as they could not by any other. But that is not their peculiar strength and satisfaction and advantage in this work. It is that their idea of God, of a divine order in the world, is such as to enable them to wait for results which, though not immediate or of personal and individual value, are incomparably desirable and important. While one type of religion, the most common of all, must have religious results first and foremost, religious education before other education, religious perfection before domestic and social decency or comfort; there is a religious spirit, a belief in the divine order which reverses the demand—which says education, plenty of it, before religious education, social improvement, civilization before salvation by faith—I don't mean in point of value, but in point of time. First, that which is natural, rational, human; then that which is spiritual. What is done well to-day is well done for ever, as much so in the household duties of a woman whose household duties are mostly drudgery and not paid because not valued, as in the sphere of a man in public life whose responsibilities are so honourable that to put a price upon them would be to insult him. It is so much of a contribution to the well-being and progress of society. Being taken up into the life of humanity, its effects not only outlive the individual, but, one way and another, must survive the race itself, and go out into space, wherever God is. If there is anything in the world of a divine presence, a divine order, this is part of the reality of it. Hence, those to whom this order is most of a reality should be best able to feel, and to rejoice in feeling that work which needs to be done for the world of a secular sort, and which, because it is secular, other people won't undertake, it depends on them to do and to get done.

"Prepare ye in the wilderness a highway for our God; make straight in the desert His paths." In this, possibly, rather than in any other form, there comes the divine call to those in every age, and specially in this age, to whom the divine order is most of a reality and a power. Personal piety— you must have much of that, say the professors of ecclesiastical engineering and pedagogy—you must have much of that before entering upon this or that work—preaching, teaching in Sunday schools, tract distribution, missions to the sick or the dissolute. It is quite true; personal piety you must have to be fit to live, not to say to teach others or help others to live well. That does not need to be said. But if you have piety enough, faith enough toward God and toward man, to have any satisfaction in helping to leave the world a little better than you have found it, for one human being or for many, then that is enough of a qualification and commission for taking part in work which will occupy your whole life, which lies at hand, which is part of your daily routine, which, though it has little or nothing to do with religious offices, is none the less the best and highest and most useful work that you can do for God or man.

This general view of the divine order and of the

demands which it makes upon those who are most conscious of the reality of it, suggests one or two reflections which I hasten to state as briefly as may be.

In regard to the fulfilment of the divine order, supposing it to be of the nature I have just said it is, it often happens that, while weaker agencies at work in forwarding it are recognised, greater ones, even the greatest of all, escape notice. Since the divine order is not always clear, it must often happen, in the case of lives of good men and even great men devoted to the advancement of it, that efforts to advance it have other results than those who made them contemplated—great results which they did not expect, no results where they expected great results.

The historical importance of John Baptist is only as great as it is because the historical importance of the New Testament in which his name occurs is as great as it is. Comparatively speaking, it is safe to say that as a forerunner of the founder of our religion what it was in his power to accomplish, and what he did accomplish, though it entitled him to be called a great man, was not a great work. Comparatively speaking, it was insignificant. In regard to the great world-movement of the Christian faith which was inaugurated by Christ, it was not much that was done or could be done by a voice crying in the wilderness of Judea, crying, as so many earnest voices had cried before, Repent. Something was done by that, though there is reason to believe not very much, to create or deepen in the minds of a few Jews of the time discontent with the social and political and especially the religious life about them, and so to prepare their minds for the reception of such an ideal of life as was just about to be revealed to mankind in the Parables and in the sermon on the Mount, and above all in the life and character of the prophet of Nazareth. But in comparison with what was done for the divine order in the new revelation of itself by other agencies of the time, what was thus done by one crying in the wilderness of Judea was insignificant. You have but to read the Gospels to suspect as much. You have only to take a glance at history to be sure of it. It was in almost an infinitely less degree by John's preaching in the wilderness to a handful of Jews and telling them to repent, than by all the civilized nations of the earth having been bent under the yoke of Rome, and by the empire of which Rome was the centre, that a reception was prepared for the Gospel of Christ for the new revelation of the order which is divine and eternal, and in which the history of an empire like that of Rome is but a moment. What a confusion of world-forces meets you at a glance into the field of universal history before Christ! Compared with the conflict among them, how paltry an affair the wars of the Jews for the possession or the retention of Canaan. Yet all these conflicting forces had been working for untold ages to this result—an imperial Rome, the mistress of a civilized world. There is no need to argue, what has been so often pointed out, that this vast order and unity as regards a measure of civilization was the greatest part of what was necessary for a still higher order and higher unity to assert itself on a larger scale among mankind in the revelation of what the gospel calls the kingdom of God. Not merely John Baptist preaching in the wilderness, but all the prophets of Israel before him, Israel itself in its national isolation and peculiar religious development from first to last, were indeed required to ripen the seed of higher life for mankind which was now to be sown. But a still larger operation than was necessary to mature the seed was indispensable to prepare for its reception this vast field of a world far advanced in civilization. Nobody who was concerned in that larger work was thinking of Christ, at any rate outside the narrow bounds of Judea. Not a soul among mankind, from the first Pharaoh to the first Roman emperor, from India in the east to Albion in the west, was dreaming of the kingdom of God taking a new phase in Nazareth and Judea; yet all that time, over all that space, the work was being done which was essential above all as a preparation for that kingdom to come, as it did come, in Nazareth, and as it has come in Great Britain.

It is often the less, not the greater and mightier agencies at work, which are recognised. No doubt almost every kind of enthusiasm has a tendency to run into religious enthusiasm. " Is Saul also among the prophets?" is a question which cool and impartial observers of human nature and human life have constantly occasion to put to themselves. There are thus prophets of the Gentiles as well as prophets of the Jews. I have named some of these prophets of the Gentiles already. Great men are enthusiasts. Various as its immediate object may be, their enthusiasm, has for its ultimate object the divine order. In its complexion it may be political or social, moral or scientific, rather than religious; it may have a special reference to a discovery, or an invention, or a mode of thought. But it reaches out necessarily into the great field of the divine order, and indeed some glimpse of that order is essential to its existence. It must have struck many minds in reading history and biography referring to recent times in our political history, that with regard to such questions as free trade the enthusiasm of enthusiasts has passed all bounds, mounted high into the region of song and prophecy. Perhaps some of us are tempted to smile at the idea of free trade being regarded by a man like Cobden as presaging a great deal of what has not yet been seen of the kingdom of God, of peace on earth, good will among men. If the enthusiasm of a politician or a social reformer has mounted into this region, so has that of an inventor, or a scientific thinker and discoverer. Bacon in this sense was a prophet of the Gentiles, so was Galileo, so was James Watt, so was George Stephenson. It is almost in language borrowed from the prophet Isaiah; it is certainly in a spirit exactly kindred to his, that a distinguished German savant speaks in a recent lecture on the theory of development of the effect as regards culture and religion, the coming throughout the world and for all time of what we call the kingdom of God, of the new and now generally accepted views of the order of nature. I wish I had time to quote a part of this lecture, which no one, I think, could read without admiration, or without profit. But you may take my word that the strain of it with regard to the discoveries of the order of nature which have been made in our time is not, indeed, in so many words, but exactly in substance, this, " Prepare ye in the wilderness a highway for our God; make straight in the desert his paths."

It is true, I say, that enthusiasm of every kind has a religious bent, is akin to prophecy, has within its ken that which concerns man's higher life in the kingdom of God. But enthusiasm is the property of the few. Its effect in producing a right estimate of the influence on man's higher life of other than expressly religious agencies is limited to the few What is certain with regard to the mass of mankind is, not that they make occasionally too much account of these, but that habitually they make too little or none at all. Even after deducting a great deal from what men who have devoted their lives to political or social reform, or to the advancement of discovery in the useful arts, or in the field of science, have thought and prophesied of their effects in improving and elevating mankind, it remains true that in these things, much more than in all other things put together, there is the promise for the world of that better day of which prophets of Israel and prophets of the Gentiles have dreamed dreams and seen visions. I believe, for my part, that thus Cobden and Haeckel are prophets of a new era, nearer at hand than any of us, perhaps, think, more wonderful and more glorious as regards civilization, culture, religion, the kingdom of God, than any, I will not say, that has been seen anywhere in the world, but than the most enthusiastic spirits of our race have imagined. Just such a revolution as steam and electricity have effected in human life in regard to material comfort, or one perhaps more wonderful still, is, I think with Haeckel, likely to be accomplished in regard to all that is intellectual, moral, religious. If this be so, some of us who are yet young, or in the prime of life, may live to see things as wonderful in that way as the wonders of the other kind that we have seen already.

As it is often not the mightier but the weaker agencies at work in furthering the divine order that are recognized and appreciated, so in the case of men who are more or less consciously devoted to the advancement of it, there is often a failure of insight; and they are found working for issues which they did not anticipate both in the way of failure and in the way of success. In regard to the divine order embracing the life of all that is, has been, shall be, the clearest sighted of mankind see through a glass darkly. In regard to that order, not of those who are indifferent to it or regardless of it, but of those who are zealous for it, it may often be said by the heavenly powers—"We have piped unto you and ye have not danced, we have mourned unto you and ye have not lamented." The disciples thought all was lost, though in point of fact all was gained, when their Master was crucified. The Christian world in the time of

Constantine was agreed that the triumph of the Christian faith was assured by his making it the religion of the State, though John Wesley had afterwards some reason, in his time, for thinking perhaps that more harm was done to it by that event than by all the Christian persecutions. The Christian world, all but a small part of it, was certain that the devil had broken loose in the Reformation in Germany, and few people who heard it did not devoutly believe that Luther's mother was a witch. It was not for the right of private judgment, free though pure and simple, that the Reformers were ready to shed their blood, but for freedom to search the Scriptures, and the right to subject the intellect and conscience to that guidance and authority, in other words, for the substitution of one authority over reason and conscience for another. To-day that which they valued least of the two things is valued most, at any rate, by minds kindred to theirs. We do not value the Scriptures less than they did, but we value free thought more.

John Baptist himself is not so remarkable for what he knew as for what he did not know of his own life-work and its effects. I mean, as regards the eternal order, in which he was no doubt a devout and a brave believer. As a forerunner he was nothing of a foreseer. He ran very much with his eyes shut, panting in his haste, but not knowing whither. When he heard of Jesus, he sent disciples to ask Him whether He was the One that was to come. The man whose business it was to say that He who was to come had come sent to ask if it was He, or if they were to look for another. He preached repentance out in the wilderness. His notion was that it was the sins of Israel that prevented the coming of the Messiah, that heavenly prince who was to reign in Jerusalem, over Rome and all the world. His preaching was repentance—" Repent and the King will come." When One came who was meek and lowly, a Son of Man rather than a Son of David, a friend of publicans and sinners, the forerunner of the Heavenly One could not, and did not understand that this was the Prince. In creating and intensifying dissatisfaction with the life of the time, especially the religious life of the time, John Baptist had a work to do in his preaching of repentance, and no doubt he did it well and bravely. Witness Herod's fear of him and his fear of the people on his account. But that was not the issue which he himself had in view. That which he looked for was not to be. He for whom he looked, was not to come; it never was intended that He should come.

Thus it is always, or commonly. Not only are the greater agencies at work in furthering the divine order, least recognized among the mass of men, but even among choice spirits devoted to the furthering of that order, misunderstanding as to the results of their own activity and the activity of others is more common than insight. It is perhaps on their unflinching adherence to the principles of the Reformation, or their defence of the authority of the Scriptures, or their zeal in the maintenance of evangelical doctrine against all adversaries and gainsayers—it is on this, perhaps, and the like of this that multitudes of religious minds rest their hopes of accomplishing anything, or much for the divine order. A champion of orthodoxy, if we had one of the stature of John Baptist or John Knox, would get crowds to follow him into the wilderness, or any other place he chose to go. He would have to be advertised no doubt, but that would be all that would be necessary. Nor would he need to depend for sustenance upon locusts and wild honey. If anyone could at one stroke once for all harmonize religion and science—ecclesiastical religion I mean, and Darwinian science—he would be the greatest man in Christendom, and therefore in the world. Kings and princes would be his humble servants for fear of the people. Thus stands the case as regards one class of agencies at work in furthering the divine order. That which is valued in regard to it is the old ecclesiastical machinery, creak and groan and rattle as it may. In the meantime, discredited to some extent by its association with enlightenment not always orthodox, the spirit of humanity enters from the outside into the religious world. Not only the Salvation Army, but every part of the Church militant is more or less affected by the influences of modern views of social life, and of the development of human society; and, as the result of this, in a thousand different forms it is attempted to direct the organization and the machinery of the Christian Church itself to other than strictly Church purposes—to the creation of new social conditions for whole communities.

What promise there is in this of a better era both for the Church and for the world is better seen as yet by the world, perhaps, than by the Church. The importance of the fact cannot at any rate be over-rated. Nothing is so common in religious circles, among good people, as lamentation. The good old times of religion are no more. We have fallen upon evil days. That is their complaint. It has reference to the small success which now attends all the attempts that are made to keep religious belief and religious life fixed where they were fixed in the good old times. In the meantime, religious people who are so much disposed to complain of the good old times passing away, are helping to prepare for times infinitely better than the good old times, in ways of which they are as far as possible from conceiving. They are deepening dissatisfaction with the life, even the religious life of the day, by their lamentations. That is one thing—a negative sort of thing. More positive is the effect of their keeping in their own view and that of others a certain high ideal of life, though it be not the highest of all. By contending for the faith as they do, even with unreason against reason, they are exhibiting something of an ideal of life above and beyond concern for meat and drink. In that way they do good as well as harm, perhaps more good than harm. Their efforts, often persevering and determined efforts, to ameliorate the physical and social condition of individuals and of classes, do good. The failures of their efforts again are full of instruction as to the need of something besides work like theirs to raise the fallen of our race. Their fierce contentions against the new light of science and free thought are abortive against the new light, but are useful in the way of taking it out from under a bushel and putting it on a candlestick. In all this, as far as they are concerned, not perhaps with intention, but as a fact, they are powerfully contributing to an advance of human life and human society such as the world has not seen, of which prophets of the Jews and prophets of the Gentiles, the enthusiasts of all time and all lands, have only dreamed dreams and seen visions. Compared with what they are doing in other ways, what they do for the kingdom of God in this mostly unintentional way is of infinite importance and value. They will not admit it, but it is so, and it is in this way above all that they hear and answer the voice of one crying in all time, and especially in our time, "Prepare in the wilderness a highway for our God, in the desert make straight his paths."

When this better time comes, it will not antiquate sorrow or the worst of sorrows, folly and sin. These will always be possible for man here below. And that reminds us that we have a life to live in view of our own well-being, as well as in view of the well-being and progress of mankind. But it is true with regard to this, as the example of Jesus may teach us, that to live for others, in view of the better day for them, is that one way in which we can make the best of life for ourselves, avoid sin and sorrow, gain nobleness and attain peace.

II.

DIVINE DISCONTENT: A COMMUNION SERMON.

"These that have turned the world upside down are come hither also."—Acts xvii. 6.

CONTENTMENT is what is praised in the New Testament Scriptures, but what they teach and preach is a divine discontent. And that is a part of their incomparable spiritual worth. Godliness with contentment is great gain. Contentment which is not what contentment often is, a substitute for godliness, is great gain. It is an achievement of the human spirit, and not a small one, to be able to regard with comparative indifference the outward circumstances of human life, good fortune and bad fortune, in view of the experience it is possible to have of life in a region higher than that of time and chance. Men of low degree are vanity, and great men are a lie. Never so much do they seem to be so as when we contrast the restless anxieties of either about the possession of things for which, on account of competition, the struggle must be severe to be successful with that equanimity which comes of thinking that, in comparison with other things which are not objects of competition, the whole of these things are not worth much of a struggle, or any at all. Certainly what is praised in the Christian Scriptures is this contentment. But, all the same, it is easy to see that what is preached there is the divinity of discontent—never for one's self, never for others to be satisfied with life just as it is, but always to have in view something higher, as to which, however unattainable, there should be no folding of the hands in sleep, no closing of the eyelids to slumber. It is not so much that this is the truth, seeing that it is so much preached in certain Scriptures, but what makes these Scriptures the truth which they are, is that they preach it so. At the basis of all human life which is not in and for itself a blunder, and something of a calamity, there is the irremovable conviction that it ought to be something better and higher. To account for this completely may be difficult. But it belongs to human nature,—it is not planted in it by this or that religion or system of morality; rather, as is to be seen from its being exhibited under the influence of various religions, it is part of the original stock of human nature. It is true that it is owing to the Christian religion that so much of it as is in existence is found among ourselves. But it would be no less true to say that we owe to it the existence of the Christian religion. Divine discontent, there is that in human nature, an essential, ineradicable part of it, account for it how you will—a recollection of the skies or a recollection of Eden, a perception gained through observation and comparison of things attainable with good which has yet to be attained. Whatever improvement, progress, is possible for one man or for many men is possible on this account. All improvement, all progress already on record has been due to it. It is not merely a beneficent motive force in human life and human society, it is the greatest and most potent of all. In and for itself it is a great part of the best of life; in regard to man's larger world of thought and feeling, it is the difference between dull stagnation and perpetual movement.

It is to stir up this discontent that any such union and united endeavour as there is among Christians is kept up. They that have turned the world upside down have come hither also—thank God for it—and we, with more or less goodwill and heartiness, have joined ourselves to them, we who belong to the Christian Church. Agitation is our profession. Unless we have denied the faith and mean to be the worst sort of infidels, we intend not to let things remain just as they are in human life and human society, but to have them altered, to keep on altering them for the better. As I read what is written in the Scriptures from which we derive the better part of our teaching, that is what we mean by thanking God as we do, that those who have turned the world upside down have come hither also.

To be sure—that is the pity—it would be difficult for us to prove that this is the feeling which maintains Christian union and endeavour in what strength and efficiency they still have. If we were challenged to prove it, it would be difficult to produce the proof, or rather to meet objections. For in truth the absence of this feeling is much more often to be remarked than the presence of it where you might expect to find it, that is, wherever two or three are gathered together in the name of Jesus. It is allowed, I think, to these two or three, or whatever number it may be, freely allowed to be of this or that mind in regard to what are called the questions of the day as respects science and religion and justice and politics, or anything of that sort. Mind is toll-free among Christians. But it is not permitted them at all to be of different minds, as to there being reason and occasion for satisfaction in regard to human life as long as heaven is as far off as it is at present, for example, from the centre of London or of Glasgow. It is not permissible, consistently, I mean, with any profession, even the slightest, of an adherence to the teaching of the Christian Scriptures, or of a belief in the Christian religion. Miracles they may doubt and yet not be taxed with infidelity. "Greater works than these shall ye do," Jesus himself says of his own works which are reported to us as miracles. But that they should be content with the world as it is, and ask neither for miracles nor hard work to change it for the better, is what no authority that I know of can grant to them, except custom, that most ancient birth of chaos.

Here, however, are all these people whose doings are reported in the daily journals as the most interesting and important events of the day—people contriving and toiling to change the conditions of human life, by wholesale if possible, and so to change life itself for the better—people actuated by a powerful discontent with respect to human life as it is. Ask who they are. The answer will not always be that they are Christians. It will be rather sometimes that they are, or are supposed to be, not sound in the faith. On the other hand, ask where all the Christians are and what they are about. You will learn, with regard to the great majority of them, that they are going to church with more or less regularity, and that for this reason they are so well content with themselves and with the world as it is, that they are not at any rate foremost in the business of trying to amend it. Divine discontent—there is not much of that among them. It has left them and has gone over to the social, political, and other reformers who may or may not be ostensibly Christians.

It is true, of course, that much of the beneficent activity of the time, whether it calls itself Christian or not, is in truth Christian—the greater part, if not the whole of it, inspired by Christian influences which are powerful to keep alive and active the divine discontent in human nature. It is, therefore, I admit, much more in appearance than in fact, that what union and endeavour there is among Christians has forgotten its own reason for being in existence —discontent with life as it is. But still the fact is not to be denied that, where we have much of a sort of devotion to the Christian religion, we have a great deal too little of that which is the soul of it. There is a kind of impression too common even yet, and not as much discountenanced as it should be by Christian institutions and societies, that human life is altogether too much of a bad job for much to be done in the way of mending it. That sort of impression represses the divine discontent that ought to exist. The same effect, of course, is produced by the impression, no less general, and just as little discountenanced by the churches, that what is wrong in this life can all be put right in another, that miracles which have ceased in time will begin again in eternity. Anyhow, so it is, in place of godliness, which, with discontentment, would be great gain, we have a dreadful quantity of godliness, which, with contentment, is a great loss.

Beside all the sin and misery to be deplored in the world, there is a contentment felt by the lover and well-wisher of his kind which goes both with godliness and ungodliness. It is true that as sin and misery are sometimes not without use, as, at any rate, the world would not be in its best features what it is without them; so something is to be said for the prevalence of a contentment, which is, on the whole, to be regretted rather than admired. The parochial view of life, and the class view of it, against which it is so difficult for any of us to struggle, is that which there is least to be got out of for theory or for practice. Apart from the one and the other, tried or judged or measured by almost any standard of value or enjoyment, what a miserably low level it is at which the mass of human existence is placed, above which it seems predestinated never to rise. Yet, over it all, in a fashion at which our wonder can never be too great, there broods an atmosphere of contentment. Rebellions and revolutions are repressed and become the accidents and portents of history, not because the police are effective, but on account of the facility with which masses of human beings accommodate themselves to existing circumstances and conditions, however forbidding and disgusting. If we are lovers of our kind, it is the gratitude of men, not their unthankfulness, it is the peaceable and contented submission of millions to the hardness of their lot, not the rebellious energy it provokes, which oftenest leaves us mourning. That nothing in human life should be more common than a certain measure of contentment, and even happiness, associated with experience which is only of privation and misery and degradation—this, I declare, is a phenomenon as wonderful as any in the heavens above or in the earth beneath. Unaccountable as it may be, however, what benevolent mind could wish it to be altogether otherwise? If the law of compensation which runs through all human life thus works medicinally and soothingly in its lowest circles, shall we not be thankful, without inquiring too curiously how it should be so? For the most part, or to a large extent, it is surely great gain, that, even where life is poorest and wretchedest, a mysterious contentment pervades it and makes it better worth living than, apart from experience, it could have been expected to be. Contentment there is in the world for which it is hard to account, which is not to be justified or commended altogether, or, indeed, at all, but with regard to which we cannot help feeling there is good in it, and that the world could not well get on without it.

At the same time, it is true no less that we have much contentment which ought to be replaced by a divine discontent, and it is also true that this regrettable contentment is sanctioned by religion. Think of those conditions of life in European countries which have to be thought of in accounting for the stream of emigration in this century from Europe to America and other parts of the globe, for the millions of people forced to rupture the ties which bind the poor to their homes as the rich are never bound to theirs, to go to a foreign country in search of food and shelter. What deplorable conditions these are. How much more deplorable the conditions from which there is no escape by emigration, conditions in which millions are forced to remain because they have no wings to carry them over sea, and no money to pay the passage. It is certainly not desirable that people who are born into them should be content to remain under such conditions all their lives. If there rises in them a discontent powerful enough to drive them to the nearest port and the farthest habitable shore, it would not be friendly advice to them to tell them that in whatsoever lot they find themselves, they do well therewith to be content. Yet, under these conditions, contentment is the rule rather than the exception among human beings whose bodies and souls are, after all, very much what ours are.

That contentment is strange enough. Hardly less strange perhaps is the contentment prevalent among other classes than those for whose worst ills emigration is something of a remedy. Surely there is as much need of emigration to the New Jerusalem, to something higher and better in the way of intellectual and moral and spiritual life, as much occasion for it amongst all classes of society, as there is for the congested populations of Europe dispersing themselves over the prairies of the West. Take some of the best and most useful, and therefore most enviable lives of the time, lives which represent our highest enlightenment and refinement, intellectual, moral, spiritual—use them as a measure by which to judge other lives, those of the great majority of people who follow various trades and professions six days in the week, and go to church with more or less regularity on Sundays. When any such measure is applied to it, life in all classes of society will be found for the most part to stand at a very low level indeed. It is not uncharitable to say so. There is perhaps a better measure still, and it gives the same results.

Those better moments in most men's lives in which the possibilities of a life far above what has been attained, [are present to us and quicken our emotions, are a measure by which to judge the rest of existence. The result of its application to the lives of the majority of people in all classes of society is only too truly indicated in the commonness of the feeling with men and women in middle life, that the good we would do, that we do not, and never will do now. The contentment which goes with all this is about as strange as that which broods as a kind of general atmosphere over poverty and destitution of the physical sort. Where you have not complete unconsciousness of intellectual and moral and spiritual poverty and destitution, you are apt to have submission to it as something natural and necessary. There is too much, not too little, contentment among the rich and comfortable as well as among the poor and needy. Life has its trials for us all. They vex us enough to make us wish that they were other than they are, that the world were different from what it is, even perhaps that we were absent from the body, and numbered with the just made perfect. But in spite of our trials, in spite of our shortcomings, errors of youth, mistakes and faults, and sins of riper years, most of us are on the whole not without a share of contentment which comes to us unasked with our daily bread. The type of man is after all still the commonest, in spite of progress of the species and of Christianity and what not, who, being eminently or moderately successful in his calling or occupation, occupying a respectable position in society, going to church and observing in a kind of way the ten commandments, lives on the whole a life of easy contentment, even though he has taken little or no trouble to cultivate and inform his mind, or has not risen in the course of many a struggle with the worser half of himself above the weaknesses and imperfections of his moral and spiritual nature. One or another earnest observer shall say this, and it shall not be possible to contradict him. I have heard of one man, as discontented a man as ever was in the world, though he was Dean of Westminster, with regard to whom a humble admirer of his, who lived near enough to him to be at any rate a constant observer, said that man was the likest to Jesus Christ he ever saw or heard of. But I have not heard of many men being thus remarked of by people who knew them well. It is not to be censorious to say that it is a life and character not very like that of the man of Nazareth, which is commonest in Christian societies, and which is only too well satisfied to be what it is. And religion sanctions this contentment, the religion of most of us sanctions it. It is something of a confused message which the conventional Christianity of the time brings to us from the unseen and eternal, but it can be interpreted to mean something like this—" It is an evil world at the-best, and the best that can be made of this earthly life is not much in view of the heavenly and divine. Look elsewhere, and in the meantime be as cheerful and contented as possible. What you know not now you shall know hereafter, what you are not now that you shall be." So the message may be, and so it is interpreted. Therefore it is that contentment is general, where it is obvious that a careful scrutiny of the actual conditions of life would leave no place or very little place for it.

In this contentment, as well as in that which is so strangely connected with the lot of the poor, there is something that makes it not altogether regrettable. The truth is, if you could put the divine discontent of the noblest and best and most Christ-like souls of this or any time into the lives of most commonplace men and women, it would make confusion in them worse confounded. With all that there is of imperfection and worse than imperfection in human nature and human life, and the contentment with it which is security given for imperfection not passing soon away, there is yet much more good than evil both in human nature and human life. The good increases; the evil steadily diminishes. That I believe, as I believe in God. That I take to be Christian belief, if any belief is what Christ's was. It is not to be thought of as a remedy for what is imperfect and faulty, or for what is miserable and deplorable in the conventional religious life of the time, that a divine discontent with things as they are should seize the multitude of believers, as it has seized the souls of saints and heroes and martyrs in every age and in almost every place. That remedy would be worse possibly than the disease. It is a Providence, in many respects wise and kindly, which shields the intellectual, moral, religious life of mankind to-day, from the agitations and convulsions which would possess it and master it, if to its own consciousness its limitations were suddenly revealed, so that, instead of multitudes going comfortably and contentedly to church on Sundays, you should have the like multitudes moved to repentance and amendment after the fashion of the inhabitants of Nineveh, when that strange missionary from the sea had fulfilled his mission. There is, after all, so much real good, in forms of character all imperfect, that if harm would be done, as often it would be, by removing from them their satisfaction with themselves, their rest-and-be-thankful finality in the matter of what is good and true, it is well that that satisfaction, that finality, cannot easily be disturbed.

All the same, it is true that there is no real good in life, nothing or not much of the highest and most enduring good, where there is not discontent with all the good there is. "Peace, peace, where there is no peace"—that is what the multitude in every age go on saying to themselves, and that is their misfortune. "Not as though I had already attained, either were already perfect"—that is the voice of the man here and there whose chance of life is a chance of life eternal and divine. A shifting horizon like this is what life requires, if it is to be life at all—a horizon which, make what effort to approach it you will, recedes ever the farther from you, grows ever the more distant and unapproachable. A receding heaven is heaven; a firmament is only a vault. It has its own peculiar ache and cross, this divine discontent of nobler souls with all that is, in view of that which might be and ought to be. It prompts to action for which often there is no return of pay or thanks. It makes havoc of some or many of the satisfactions and enjoyments, which are the best of commonplace lives, not merely in the case of the patriot, or the prophet of rude and lawless times, but often in the instance of neighbour and friend and citizen in peaceable society. It is often this which brings a man into collision, more or less disagreeable and painful, with vested interests, common modes of thought, old customs, churches, and other institutions no longer what they were. It is hard to reform the world without, harder still to reform the world within, that is, if you are minded to reform it thoroughly. That hard task of an ultra-radical the man assigns to himself who is possessed by this divine discontent of which I speak. Yet it is, I say, the secret, or at any rate one indispensable condition of life being real at all— of any of the highest good belonging to it. Progress or improvement there can be none without it. Not only so, there is in it, and in it alone, that perpetual play and exercise of what is best in human nature and human life, the absence of which is death. Between a contented man, a rich man, or a pious man, pious by square and rule, saying to himself, " Soul, thou hast much goods laid up for many years," and an apostle, without home, or country, or spare cash, or benefit of Habeas Corpus in insurrectionary quarters, saying to himself, " Not as though I have attained or were already perfect," the difference is that the one man lives and the other is dead even while he lives. That heaven of which pious souls have dreamed dreams and seen visions, in which every desire, even the desire to be better and higher, will be suddenly fulfilled—that glorious stagnation of being and doing—would be the exact antipodes of heaven to a man who has known here in this evil world what it is "to strive, to seek, to find, and not to yield."

It is to cultivate not contentment but discontent that the Christian Church now exists or has any right to exist. Those that have turned the world upside down have come hither also. We have joined ourselves to their society. It is the peculiarity of the institution and organization we call a church, it is what gives it what right it has to exist, that in it distinctions among men, important or essential to all other institutions, or almost all, are of no account; that it knows neither Jew nor Greek, neither bond nor free, neither rich man nor poor man—for the matter of that, neither saint nor sinner. Other institutions and societies exist because they have been called into existence by the conditions of human life, being as divergent as they are in different countries and in different ranks and classes of society. Without regard to this divergence, or, at any rate, taking account of it only for a peculiar purpose, our society exists for this above all other objects, to bring whatever is in human life to the test of what is the best and highest. In this one institution we are not hampered as the members of other institutions are hampered by conventionalities and traditions, the authority of which it is impossible to distrust without shattering the institutions. Our object in this one institution, if I understand it rightly, is with perfect freedom from prepossessions in favour of what is, to bring everything to the test of what ought to be—that test which is given in the spirit of man as the one true source of all truth, all revelation, all religion. It is to the heart that Jesus refers all questions of life and duty, of what ought to be as compared with what is; and we preserve, or profess to preserve, in this institution the tradition of the method of Jesus. Anyhow, this is the test to which we bring all things. To bring all things to this test is the object for which, as a Christian society, we exist. The Church exists to cultivate not contentment—of which so many of its members have too large a share already—but discontent, divine discontent, of which we can never have enough. The true invisible Church inside and outside of the visible one, is a society of malcontents, people who would turn the world upside down again after the fashion of those poor men who began to revolutionize the Roman Empire, not in the interests of the poor and needy, but in favour of the soul that loves righteousness. In the character of Christ Himself, in the kindred spirituality of the writings of His immediate disciples and followers, in the enlightened thought of all past ages, and now of our own, an ideal of life has gained for us a certain consistency and definiteness of outline which enables us to speak of it as Christian, and to be understood when we so speak of it. I do not know why we should be associated as we are together in what we call a church, if it is not with reference to this ideal, to take account of what is conformable and what is unconformed to it in our own lives and the lives of others, with the inevitable effect—for the effect, I should say, is inevitable—of only the dull and undiscerning saying "Peace, peace," and all the wise and clear-sighted saying, "Not as though we had already attained or were already perfect." Bring all that is in human life at this moment to the test of its being or not being what the best and highest in human nature at this moment could wish it to be; that is, do what you mean to do in being a member of a society like this; and if that means anything, it means that a divine discontent is the life and soul of such a society. It is true that this is an ideal Church. The actual one is different, so different that the existence of the Church, and not merely some of its activities, is called into question. It is an ideal. But it is one—there is this to be said of it—which has the power to re-assert itself as often as it is forgotten and displaced. It is true, too, that in this way, as an institution, the Church has its limitations which it is not easy to see that it can ever overpass. It cannot always undertake the reforms which it brings into view. Part of its discontent must be that its discontent is unavailing, impracticable. We cannot as a society assail directly all the hindrances and obstructions, the evils and calamities, which make it impossible for multitudes of human beings to have any experience of that life which to us is life indeed. We cannot even undertake to point out the exact method by which these hindrances and obstructions, evils and calamities, may be removed. But for all that, in spite of its being subject to such limitations, the society to which we belong, as far as it is a society for the cultivation of a divine discontent with that which is, is not the least practical of institutions, apart altogether from what it has ever done, or means to do, in the way of practical beneficence. Godliness with discontentment is great gain to the world and to the individual man, in for ever provoking the effort to be and to do something better and higher than that which is or has been done. Take as your example of this divine discontent Him, in looking to whom so many of the best and noblest of our race have learned to live not unto themselves. It was with reference to what His own heart had to tell Him of the best that might be, and that should be, that there rose in Him that discontent with what was—Mosaism, Pharisaism, Sadduceeism—that discontent of which He foresaw the end, the end of which we know, the end which is remembered by us in a special rite this day. It is good to belong to a society in which discontent like His is what is, or ought to be, cultivated, and in which those Scriptures are sacred, that praise contentment indeed, but preach discontent.

III.

THE CARCASE AND THE EAGLES.

"Wheresoever the carcase is, there will the eagles be gathered together."—Matthew xxiv. 28.

"GOD in history" is not a new idea, if what is meant is God occasionally or frequently interposing in human affairs. In that sense, so far from being a new idea, it is as old as the very oldest histories. But in the sense that there is law and order in the sphere of human life, as elsewhere throughout the universe, it is so. Such breadth and precision have been given to it in our times as to make it virtually a new idea. The habit of looking at things in their causes and sequences was exceptional among ancient historians. It is the rule among historians now.

It is curious and interesting to notice how much of the recorded thought of Jesus is, in this respect, an anticipation of modern habits of thought. It is especially curious and interesting, I think, to notice how much of it is of this character as regards that part of human life, in respect to which our modern view of things has encountered the greatest resistance in the common mind—in regard, that is to say, to what is terrible, awful, stupendous in the way of calamity. It is much less common, I should say, in the religious world of to-day to meet with an intelligent and hearty recognition of law and order in human affairs, as they are shown in the constant and gradual improvement and elevation of the human race, than to find a tendency to recognise a God, usually far off, as unmistakably present in a tremendous conflagration, a fearful deluge, a great plague, a battle resulting in prodigious slaughter. It has always been less common to find the presence of God observed and noted in the beneficent operations of nature, in the daily course of the sun, than in the appearance in the midnight sky of a comet "with fear of change perplexing monarchs." It is especially noticeable, therefore, that in regard to this part of human life, as in regard to every other, the recorded teaching of the Author of our faith is so complete an anticipation of our modern habits of thought.

Take, for example, that saying of his, "Wheresoever the carcase is, there will the eagles be gathered together." It is not, I believe, to forget or underrate any or all of the astonishing discoveries which have rewarded the toil and patience and genius of the great lights of modern science and philosophy, to say that we have in this saying of the Master the clearest, most powerful, most penetrating glance that was ever at any one moment in history directed to the divine order of the world. Suppose him to be speaking of the last days before the coming of the Son of Man, and having much to say of calamities, tribulations, judgments, famines, pestilences, wars, as belonging to those days, and suppose some one, interrupting him, to ask, "When shall these things be? When will they happen—this year, or next, or not for a dozen, or a hundred, or a thousand years?" You can imagine that question being put by one who conceived that they might happen at any time—just as God willed. And this was Christ's answer, "Wheresoever the carcase is, there will the eagles be gathered together,"—an answer which looks the vaguest possible, but the precision of which is a marvel; for it means that the things in question do not at all happen, that is to say, fall out anyhow or anywhere as God wills, but that they arise in the way of cause and effect, of invariable, inevitable sequence, at one time and one place and at no others. It is an answer, therefore, which I say is an anticipation, and a wonderful one, of the modern spirit which looks at things in the light of a divine and eternal order of the world.

I need hardly say that it is often a morbid feeling

in which the tendency to talk about the darker side of human life takes its rise and to which it is congenial. Certainly it is a morbid feeling, to the prevalence of which it is due, that there are still minds that see more of the Invisible in a pestilence, a war, a year of dull trade, the potato rot, murders in Ireland, an event that eclipses the gaiety of nations than in a great discovery in science, the invention of the printing press or the steam engine, commercial prosperity—any event or series of events by which the well-being of individuals or of nations is promoted or the progress of the race accelerated. If it were not sad, it would be grotesque and ridiculous, to think not of an individual here or there, but of large masses of human beings forgetting God except when they are reminded of His existence by being suddenly knocked down. A judgment here, another there, and still another yonder—why, what a life they would make for us if we were to attend to all that some good people, believers in a good God, have to say of it! If they had their way they would make no more kindly a home for some of us whose dispositions are not heroic, than timid landlords find in a country in which agrarian disturbances are rife, and in which, behind every hedge and in every ditch, there may be supposed to lurk an armed miscreant intent on bloodshed. "Great is the Lord," they would have us sing in untuneful chorus, "great is the Lord and greatly is He to be suspected."

It is a different thing to look at the darker side of human history and human life in the light of the divine order, not as presenting God occasionally to view in a startling and dreadful manner, but as part of that revelation of Himself which is made to the thinking mind by the world, visible and invisible, and which, to the best thought of the best minds, has ever been provocative of wonder and admiration.

It can never be exactly an inviting or enjoyable, though it is often a salutary mental occupation to make a study of calamity, disaster, all that is blackest and darkest in the page of history. The preacher who has a turn for brooding over all this is a sort of ghoul, and might perhaps be called to exercise his function rather more appropriately in the churchyard than in the church. At the same time, it is not a small part of human history or human experience which is of this nature, and to ignore the fact would be still more senseless than to brood over it. It can never be an inviting, though it may be an instructive, study. If you fling on it the light which there is in the recorded thought of the great Teacher, and especially in this one saying of His, the result must be to show that the forces of destruction balance other forces in the sphere of human life, are needed to do it, and that

III. THE CARCASE AND THE EAGLES.

thus it is not one part merely of the divine order, but the whole of it which is beneficent. In a word, the man who asks with regard to all that men and nations have most reason to dread and fear, "When shall these things be?"—who asks this question with any hope of gratifying a morbid craving for the sensational, such as belongs to the chapter of frightful accidents, is under a hallucination as to the order of the world in which he lives, or rather is mistaken in supposing, as he virtually does, that there is no such order.

As every one knows, whether he has been a traveller himself or has only read the accounts of travellers, it is astonishing in eastern and tropical countries to see how instantaneously the vulture pounces upon the carcase. What is astonishing on land is still more astonishing at sea, as every one on board ship on a voyage in the South Pacific must often have noticed—silence and solitude in the heavens above and the sea beneath—one vast resplendent solitude answering to another. You look to sky and sea, above, around, and feel that in that vast transparency nothing can be hid, not even a gnat's wing, for hundreds of miles. But if a dead cat or a piece of meat is thrown overboard, almost it would seem in an instant the albatross, the vulture of the sea, or some of his kin, has dropped out of the sky upon it, and has to fight for the possession of it with a score or a hundred of competitors.

"Wheresoever the carcase is, there will be the eagles gathered together." The muster does not take place by chance here, there, anywhere, but it must take place just then and there. It is just as sure as that the soul of things, the good that is in them, goes out of them, that dissolution and destruction begin to operate upon them. The sanatory arrangements of the universe are as wonderful as any other. It is in fact involved in that law of progress which is the law of human society, that growth, increase, development of what is good and useful should be accompanied by dissolution and destruction of what is the opposite. That which lives in the sphere of human affairs is the natural antagonist, the destroyer, vulture of that which is dead, or ought to be so. There are other causes at work to this effect, but this is one.

It is in this point of view that it is so significant to find Jesus forecasting in connection with the new doctrine of peace on earth, good-will among men, not peace but a sword—not an immediate millennium but tribulations, disasters, convulsions such as the world had not seen before. Every step in advance, much more, every great step in the progress of civilization, culture, religion, by necessity of the case, involves the dissolution and destruction of what has hindered it and is incompatible with it. God is not a God of the dead but of the living—not merely not *of* the dead but *against* the dead, and for that we are the living to praise him.

Nothing, not even gunpowder or dynamite, is so destructive as an idea, if only it be a good idea. Nothing in the sphere of human life and human history is so much solvent of the worst as a touch of the best. What is good in this sphere only keeps its life till that which is better comes, and then there is nothing for it but death and dissolution. Let in a little light, or, as it has been called, a little lucidity, into the sphere of human things, and, as sure as fate, whole forests and thickets of error, unreason, superstition, misbelief, not only droop and pine, but rot and beg for destruction.

This comes of that struggle for existence in which men have their part to play, of the stern necessity there is for human life to make the most and the best it can of itself and its surroundings. A man might write a treatise, rather than a sermon, on this subject and call it a history of civilization—with an appendix concerning the true religion. In the sphere of human life, I repeat, that which is the life of things is their use. When that is spent, all things else conspire to have them not only disabled but abolished. On sea and land where man is not, it may be only contingent, though usual, that where the carcase is, there the eagles are gathered together; but where man is, it is certain.

Steam and electricity are new ideas, new forces by which man has extended his command over material resources indispensable for his existence. As surely as these new ideas are introduced, there is found to be implied in them destruction as well as creation. A host of things in which there was life because there was use become refuse and old lumber,—handlooms, wooden ships, mail coaches,—and with regard to them the question is how they are to be got rid of. A new gun is invented in America or in England, and all the stands of arms in all places of arms throughout the world become lumber until they have undergone a process of conversion which is a process of destruction.

Belshazzar's feast is not a spectacle pleasing to gods or men, that small part of mankind excepted for whom the lights flare upon rude riot and excess. It may be a product of civilization and of national struggles and aspirations. It is not exuberant life, but rampant disease and corruption, and as such it is marked for dissolution and destruction. Always when it is at its height there is to be seen the handwriting on the wall, telling that tyranny and oppression have but their day, that they are weighed in the balance and found wanting, that the next thing to heedless excess is destruction. The doctrine of constitutional liberty gains a footing in a country ignorant of it before—the result, if not at once, inevitably is, that institutions, laws, privileges, class distinctions, offices and officers, lose what vitality they had, and with regard to them, as with regard to all that is dead, the question is, what is the swiftest and most effectual method of destruction.

In every department of human life the same process is at work, that which lives and grows necessitating the dissolution and removal of that which is useless and corrupt. In this view of it, the process is a necessary part of the fulfilment of the divine order on the side of progress and improvement. It is beneficent. That which so often makes it seem other than beneficent—and this too has to be recognised as a fact—is the redundance of vested interests—it is that in so many instances the interests and affections of men and nations are linked rather with what may have been once good than with that which being better is destined to dissolve and to replace it. This is why destruction which goes along with creation is so often a painful and terrible experience. It is not unfortunate or unnecessary for mankind that Belshazzar and his courtiers should have but their day, or rather their night; but, when the handwriting on the wall makes its appearance, the mighty king and his court cannot well be expected to welcome it. There is comfort and satisfaction for a benevolent and thoughtful mind in the reflection that the sanatory arrangements of the universe are as wonderful as any of the other arrangements in it; but for men and nations whose habits and feelings are involved in the existence and perpetuation of what is opposed to them and inconsistent with them, these arrangements cannot but be felt to act often in a harsh, peremptory, ruthless, unsparing manner.

It is well however to accustom ourselves to look at them in the proper light, namely as beneficent, not only that we may not miss or misread a great deal which is written for our learning in the pages of history, but that in the changing fashions of our theology we may be always mindful of one thing, to recognise God as not a God of the dead but of the living. Only some scattered hints can be thrown out on a subject which is far too large to be adequately discussed here and now.

Having said that it is in the first place and above all in one way, namely, in the course of human progress and enlightenment, in the natural growth and increase of what is most alive because most useful and beneficial, that much in the sphere of human life and human society loses its vitality and becomes a prey to destruction, I must add that in other ways the same result is assured, especially in the way opposite to the natural growth of good, namely, the natural growth of evil. Good is a solvent of the worst—the most powerful of all solvents. So is the worst a solvent of that which is evil, or not the best. It is a part of the eternal order of the world for that which is good to operate in the destruction of that which is opposite to itself: the greater the good the greater the destruction. So it is no less a part of the eternal order that the forces at work in the sphere of human things, if ungoverned or misgoverned with reference to that order, operate also in the way of destruction. There are combinations of atoms which under certain conditions are quiescent, harmless—in a solid form they can be handled with safety, in the form of fluid or gas they are irresistibly destructive. Considering what man is on the one hand, and what on the other are his surroundings in the universe, much that finds a place in human life and human society is of this character; the latent force in it under certain natural conditions has only to be developed to prove destructive.

This is one of the great lessons of history and of the Bible, which is partly history. It is one of which, as a rule, we are less mindful in the Christian Church, not only than we ought to be, but less mindful than people were accustomed to be in our own branch of the Christian Church centuries ago. It is a set-off of its kind, and not an inconsiderable set-off, to the harsh theology of the Reformation preachers and leaders that they were every one of them, or almost every one, addicted to reflecting and discoursing much upon the question, not what must *I* do to be saved, but what must *we* do—what must the nation and other nations do to be saved? Often, it is true, the harsh theology of the men of the Reformation dictated a harsh and repulsive estimate of the character and destiny of nations and of mankind, but it is to their credit that, such as it was, an estimate of that sort was a great part of their preaching. It is a meagre as well as a hypochondriacal religious and social life which is nourished among us in some quarters by preaching which is a stereotyped rejoinder to the question What must *I* do to be saved? or which has no outlook upon mankind except backwards upon Judea and beyond that to the Egypt of the Pharaohs and to Noah's ark.

What is read and thought inside the Christian Church, I mean on the subject of the teaching of history, man's wonderful experience in this best or worst of all worlds, is what is read and expounded in church piece-meal on Sundays, here a little and there a little, and altogether very little indeed—what is written in the Bible, that is to say, and no more. And that certainly cannot be too highly valued. As far as it goes it is incomparably instructive. Yet I will venture to say that religious education, if not among boys and girls at school, certainly among children of a larger growth of this generation, is not what it ought to be; religious thought lacks more than it contains of one invaluable element when people have only read the Books of Kings and Chronicles and have not opened a book to see what is meant by the Decline and Fall of the Roman Empire or the French Revolution.

These are two great epochs in the history of mankind, epochs of destruction and construction. It was never intended by Providence, I am sure, that all that relates to them should be for religious people in this century anxious to acquaint themselves with the divine order in the world, thrown into the background, and, indeed, marked lumber or contraband by comparison with accounts in Kings and Chronicles of the wars of the Jews with each other and with the surrounding tribes and nations. Read Gibbon, and you see how in the prodigious organization of the Roman Empire, which was so indispensable a preparation for the diffusion of the Christian religion, all that was once good and living was turned to its opposite, all that was originally crude or vicious in its conflict with the laws of Nature and of God was enormously developed, and in its conflict with them was reduced to helplessness and rottenness. Then you see on every side as far as the eye can range, not the barbarians only, but all that was living and aggressive in the world conspiring and combining to have the enormous carcase riven in pieces and dispatched. There never was such a carcase under heaven before, or such a muster of the eagles.

It is the same picture, perhaps on a smaller scale, in the history of the French Revolution. Read Carlyle, and see what was good in courts, laws, institutions, social gradations, refinement of manners, religion, turned to its opposite, and therefore as good as dead, or worse than dead. What a mass of antagonisms, in their origin and in the first place violations of the eternal order, but in the second place recriminative and mutually destructive; what an array of such antagonisms are at work with an issue as terrible as it was unforeseen. There the carcase was, and there the eagles were gathered together.

Look again at slavery in America. There, too, as in the decline and fall of the Roman Empire and in the French Revolution, in the antagonisms of national life arising inevitably out of the life of a people ungoverned or misgoverned, there as regards the eternal order of the world was the carcase, and there the eagles were gathered together.

It is the same lesson which is to be learned from the history of these periods as history is now written, which is taught in the books of Chronicles and Kings, when you read that Rehoboam or Jeroboam or Ahab did that which was evil in the sight of the Lord, and brought down upon himself and upon the people along with him the horrors of pestilence, famine, war, rebellion. But with reference to the intricate conditions of human life, rational life, in modern as compared with ancient times, the lesson is enforced in these histories in a different manner from that in which it was possible for a Jewish annalist to teach it.

In all these instances good came out of evil. The sanatory arrangements of the universe are wonderful. So far it is not difficult to see how it is possible to justify the ways of God to man, to vindicate the eternal order from the suspicion of being needlessly relentless. The first lesson which is taught by these instances, at any rate that which is first demonstrated by them is that, if evil is good in the making, part of the process finds its explanation in the nature of evil as compounded of elements mutually repulsive. That which is in harmony with the eternal order, which experience therefore calls good, is in harmony with itself, and its existence and growth are assured by that harmony. That which is out of harmony with the same order, called evil because it has been found to be so, is in conflict with itself as well as with all that is, and is therefore up to the limits of its growth and increase, and in proportion to its growth and increase, self-destructive. Good is a solvent of evil, evil is a solvent of itself. This is one of the great lessons of history and of the revelation of God in history; and we have not learned much till we have learned it.

I have said too much upon this point, considering the time at my disposal, though perhaps I could hardly have said less. One does not need to be an alarmist to see or to acknowledge that we ourselves live in critical times, in which the lessons of history that are taught as clearly as this is ought not to be disregarded. God is not a God of dead nations like the Hebrews, but of the living like our own and others with which we have relations of amity or antagonism. Politics are perhaps foreign to the pulpit, but history is not so, not even the history of Turkey or the history of Russia. It is evident that the state of things in one of these countries—I mean in Russia—is critical, and even alarming. What we know of that country would seem to point unmistakeably to the conclusion with regard to its present condition, that, be the constitution of the Government right or wrong, so much of civilization has entered into the life of the people that now much of what organization has been provided for it is found to be in conflict with itself, because more or less in conflict with the ascertained conditions of human well-being and progress, with the eternal order of the world. Where life and growth ought to be you have decay and corruption and the necessity, or at any rate the origin, of Nihilism, that terrible eagle which under other names has so often astonished mankind by appearing where it was not looked for.

It is no less evident than anything with regard to the condition of Russia that in our own country as well as in most European countries at the present moment, that is to say throughout the civilized world, a movement of a critical kind is in progress and is always gathering volume and force to alter, if not subvert, existing social and political conditions and arrangements in regard to the relations of class to class—of the rich to the poor, the titled to the untitled, the capitalist to the labourer, the owner of land to the landless and penniless, in short, of the educated, governing, privileged few to the misgoverned, neglected, ill-starred many. It is a movement which is not to be checked or vetoed, we may be sure, by Parliamentary tactics, by one political party saying to another, "Thus far shalt thou go and no farther," or by platitudinarian preachers, preaching at so much a quarter the good old gospel of every man being bound to be content with the lot in which Providence has been pleased to place him. The question with regard to this movement is whether or not there is in it any indication or proof that in the present organization of society, here and elsewhere, there is included much which at any rate in this age belongs not to civilization and Christianity, but to barbarism and heathenism, much which is antiquated and pernicious. If in that organization much of this nature is included, it is as good as under sentence of death, and the dissolution of it is a foregone conclusion.

All this might be applied to special institutions, customs, modes of thought, of which I have no time to say anything. I can only name for your consideration one or two examples in which the application of it is a simple affair.

It is a question with a great many different sorts of people, actuated by different motives, how long the Church will last or whether it will last for ever. That is so large a question, especially considering the wide diversity of signification which belongs to the word Church, that I shall not enter into it at length. Take, however, a particular Church, one too well known to need description, our own for example, and ask the question with regard to that. Not much time or reflection is needed to answer it. Of course the Church in this sense would not be abolished though it were disestablished to-morrow. In that view there is no need to ask whether the disestablishment eagles that have gathered together are genuine eagles or sham eagles, artificial kites hoisted into the air to frighten the partridges. We don't need to ask that question. The question with regard to the existence of the Church, which has been of use else it would not have lived so long, is whether in its present form it has still in it any or much of the vital force of use and profit—not use and wont. I should say from my reading of history, and of the Bible too, that a Church once alive in that respect might go defunct, and then we know, from Scripture and from history, how long it could last and what would become of it.

It is what gives Churches—I am not speaking of course of the invisible but of the visible Church—it is what gives Churches as well as other institutions their lease of life, longer or shorter as the case may be, that their life is commonly a mixed quantity, includes use and profit along with use and wont, even use and wont with a resemblance to original sin or a likeness to total depravity. There are always eagles, ground eagles, screaming destruction to all that is ancient, conventional, customary—Churches among the rest of human things. If there were Churches which only or chiefly or at all sought to arrest the progress of enlightenment, to meddle mischievously with man's vested interest in truth and light, or which proposed to themselves as their loftiest aim perfection in the matter of Church millinery, doctrine *à la mode*, posture and imposture, and did not help to clothe the naked and to feed the hungry, and as regards the moral and spiritual universe open the eyes of the blind, they would not long be cumberers of the ground.

Turn from an institution like the Church to consider for a moment a mode of thought. You can see from what I have been saying of the sanatory arrangements of the universe, what is the meaning of ordaining a fast-day to arrest the ravages of a pestilence. An eminent statesman, now no more, would not have given so much offence in our day as he did at the time by recommending the well-meaning people of this city who begged him to proclaim a fast in view of the spread of cholera, to study cleanliness in reference to the conditions of towns and cities, to remember that dirt was matter in the wrong place. We understand all that better now than it was understood thirty or forty years ago. We know that where there is matter in the wrong place the consequences of that misplacement are not to be obviated or restricted but in one way, not by fasting and prayer which are spiritual acts, but by sanatory labour well directed. To us accordingly, I suppose, the meaning of a fast intended to stop the cholera might be expressed by saying that it is to put up a scarecrow to terrify the eagles. Here in fact we have an instance of a mode of thought, once lively enough, now defunct, the soul of which was about to depart thirty years ago and has since departed, and which all the activity of the human mind in every department of its labour and striving is as fast as possible resolving into nothingness.

Like this one, many older modes of thought are a prey to destruction in presence of that which is truer and better than themselves. It does not matter that so many books have been written and so many earnest discourses preached to show that a man is to be saved, that his destiny as a rational creature is to be determined here and hereafter by renouncing the use of his reason in order to believe what his reason either does not tell him to believe or tells him not to believe. That is a mode of thought out of which the life that was in it has for the most part departed, just because something better and truer has entered into the common thought of the race, just because we have been led in many ways, by many paths, to believe so much more than it was believed once, that a man is saved and his destiny is fixed, not indeed by the works of the law, but by believing with all his heart that which to a good and pure heart was never doubtful since time began. That older mode of thought in presence of this newer, the new being better than the old, loses its vitality in spite of all endeavours to coddle it, and is undergoing decay and dissolution.

In all this, what has been said has been said of judgment, retribution, calamity, destruction, all the darker and darkest side of human life and human history. The outcome of it all as regards the individual man is that he should learn or suspect that there is a chance, or rather certainty, absolute certainty, of one result from the association of his interests and his affections and his activity with the baser and worse part of life, the result, namely, of calamity, judgment, retribution, call it what you please, occurring to him. In regard to these sanatory arrangements of the universe God is no respecter of persons. Hell and the devil are figures of speech, just as the eagles of which I have been speaking are metaphorical. But they mean much, the meaning of which is more rather than less in an age like ours in which they are taken for what they are. On the side of what is good and on the side of what is evil, of what is in harmony and what is out of harmony with the divine eternal order, the possibilities of human nature, of human life, for the individual man as for the race, are vast, incalculable, sublime. Here, too, the forces of destruction balance those of production and creation on a scale which is sublime. Just because there is in every man a higher as well as a lower nature—good in that sense as well as evil—disorder, confusion, conflict, are possible in every life, certain if the lower nature usurps the place of the higher, if good grows not, lives not, and if evil lives and grows. Look at the drunkard, the liar, the sensualist, the hypocrite, the slave driver, the slave of ignorance, the slave of greed or envy. It is the disorder and confusion and degradation which are certain in the inward life of the man, not that which is contingent in his outer life, that is of the nature of calamity, judgment, retribution. That is where the carcase is, and where the eagles are gathered together.

This is true and it is full of warning. Yet, I think that in that view of the darker side of human life which it is possible for a thoughtful and benevolent mind to take, the feeling which must finally prevail over every other in regard to it is not that of the alarmist or the dogmatist who is awed by the expectation of chaos coming again, or who shudders at the idea of falling unawares, perhaps through sudden death, into the hands of the living

God. It is rather the feeling of a believer in an order which is divine and eternal, which in reference to evil as in reference to good is wonderful in its working, the destruction belonging to which is beneficent, the severity of which is kindness. "Thy mercy is in the heavens, thy faithfulness reacheth unto the clouds. Thy righteousness is like the great mountains. Thy judgments are a great deep. How excellent is thy loving kindness, O Lord; therefore the sons of men put their trust under the shadow of thy wings."

IV.

METHODS OF SPIRITUAL TREATMENT.

"Suffered many things of many physicians."—Mark v. 26.

TWELVE years, according to this narrative, this woman was under the care of physicians, and twelve years are no small of part human existence. For a considerable part of this mortal life her effort had been with their help merely to live; she had suffered many things of many of them, and had spent her whole living upon them, with the result that she was nothing bettered but rather grew worse. Medical treatment is often unavailing, because medical science and skill have to contend, in many instances or most, not only with disease but with stupidity, not only with the distemper of patients but with their ignorance and carelessness. But at any rate cases like this are not rare in which ample leisure is given to observers to consider how unavailing it is. How often have we not heard the same story as we read here, of the elaborate futility, under certain conditions, of medical practice. Day after day the patient goes to his doctor, hoping for relief from his sufferings, if not for restoration to health, all the while perhaps doing his best to frustrate the efforts which are made on his behalf; he has new and again new remedies tried upon him from which much is expected and nothing is gained; in despair of being cured by one physician, he tries another; turns from the doctor to the quack, and from the quack back to the doctor, till at last possibly there is no hiding from himself the truth which has long been palpable to others, that his case is hopeless, and that for him physicians and physic are of no avail.

If there is a suggestion, however, lurking in the narrative as to the occasional futility of medical treatment, still more significant is the fact on which it lays stress that, whether or not this patient had suffered much from her plague, she had at any rate suffered many things of many physicians.

Except by curious inquirers little is known now of what patients have had to suffer beyond and above what nature meant they should endure. At present in this country and other European countries much is done by medical skill, if not to conquer disease, certainly to alleviate pain. The whole tendency of medical practice, as we know anything of it, is in the direction of carefully minimizing suffering. But possibly, taking the whole history of the world into view, speaking of the experience of all ages and all nations, we might have to admit that it is questionable whether the sum of human misery and agony has not been increased rather than diminished by physicians. Until modern modes of thought and investigation served to demonstrate their futility and absurdity, the most arbitrary and violent methods of arresting and alleviating disease were those which were everywhere in vogue. Until comparatively recent times, even in the most enlightened countries of Europe, bleeding and blistering, the actual cautery, liberal doses of the most nauseous, most powerful, most poisonous drugs, were the chief resources of the ordinary medical practitioner. He was dogmatic in his conviction that, when anything is wrong in the human body, nature must be forced by violence to put it right, and his patient had often to suffer more from him than from fevers or wounds. All these arbitrary and violent modes of medical practice are obsolete except in the East—where no anguish compares with that connected with the disturbance of a custom or any change of ideas. Elsewhere they are recognized as irrational and absurd, and denounced as barbarous and even inhuman. There are cases in which the physician must still, to save life, resort to treatment which is painful. But it is now known, it is now conclusively settled among physicians, that the way to master disease is not to torture the patient into health or into his grave, but to provide that those miraculous processes of nature which include healing should as far as possible have fair play, to make art the handmaid of nature, instead of offering any violence to nature in the name of art. Now-a-days, therefore, your physician who is not an age behind his age does not give you drugs in doses which horribly aggravate your suffering—he prescribes fresh air, the delights of travel, gentle exercise, good diet, warmth, comfort, suggests that pleasant company has its own benign influence on body and mind, recommends innocent amusement, and, as regards the welfare of this mortal tabernacle, agrees with the ancient maxim that godliness with contentment is great gain. It is certain that more cures are effected by the modern system of medical treatment, while, as for the soothing of pain, no comparison is possible between them. The difference between the two systems is that by the one the attempt is made to check and to extirpate disease by violence, by the other to aid nature by gentle methods to overcome it.

From doctors for the body is not the passage easy to doctors for the soul? Among them, too, the curing of disease by violence has been much and long in vogue. In our day, it is true, we hear little and know less of the coarser and more outrageous means which were once universally approved for effecting spiritual cures. We don't now believe that we can save souls by burning the bodies belonging to them. The mode of thought, to which it seemed possible or likely that by sending a troop of drunken dragoons into a quiet village on a Sunday morning and putting the inhabitants to the sword, the condition and the prospects of the kingdom of God might be improved in the neighbourhood has become obsolete. The civil magistrate among us does not exercise his powers as a terror to evil-doers at the bidding of any ecclesiastical dictator or committee or corporation. We have so far reduced the doctrine of toleration to practice that we no longer resort to the infliction of political disabilities and the use of legal penalties in order to repress dissent and to quash heresy. But, as we know, these methods of spiritual treatment were once universally approved throughout the Christian world. John Calvin believed in them as much as the most scandalous of the popes or the most ruthless of Christian kings and emperors. Skill and courage in the application of them were celebrated in verse and commemorated in marble, as we now honour great statesmanship or distinguished philanthropy. The man who did not believe in them was to his age and country a Laodicean, a Gallio, a man of Belial, a son of perdition. We hear little now of the preaching of condemnation, the agonies of the damned in hell do not now echo wherever two or three are gathered together in the name of the merciful Son of Mary. But it is not long since this was believed to be the only faithful preaching of the gospel and the only way to save souls. There are opposite methods in theology as in medicine; the older is manifestly giving place to a newer, if not a better. We may regret the change, but at all events we cannot dispute it. In general the old way in theology as in medicine was arbitrary, harsh, violent. Its motto was "kill or cure." According to the conceptions of revealed truth upon which it proceeded, revelation has been added to experience, divine light has superseded the light of nature, to give us the most hopeless and dismal view of the world and life, of human nature and human destiny. According to the view which it gives you of the religion of Christ, you can only understand Christianity by approaching it through an older religion, which it was destined, not to improve, but to supersede. Its Christianity looks down upon you from Sinai, and its colossal features are cut in the image of the Jew. Compare the harshness of the Mosaic religion with the mildness of the Christianity of Christ. In general, if you look at the older religion of the Bible, you see that it deals with human nature harshly and violently, not merely using terror as its main instrument, but banishing nature from nature, twisting human life into artificial shapes and forms, so that when its stern code of laws is ever so strictly obeyed, the man who has obeyed it is not necessarily a righteous man, a good man, a man of sound moral and spiritual nature, but only a respectable or regimental Jew. Does not St. Paul harp upon this in all his writings, telling us in a hundred ways, under a hundred different figures of speech, that the law was a system of bleeding and blistering, actual cautery, caustic and drastic drugs applied to the spiritual man, with only the effect in most cases of making him worse instead of better?

In spite of the contrast which Judaism thus offers to the Christianity of Christ, the newer religion has been assimilated wonderfully to the older. That form of Christianity with which the world hitherto has been more familiar than with any other is one in which there is more of the spirit of Deuteronomy and Leviticus than of the sermon on the Mount, or the good Samaritan, or the Prodigal Son. To please God, that awful censor who sees you and knows you without knowing your frame and remembering that you are dust, you must hate the world, abhor and renounce everything which makes youth glad and age cheerful and life tolerable, you must not be natural, you must keep down or cut out as much as possible all human desires and feelings, you must not take too much pleasure in your children or your friends, for God is a jealous God and may cut them off to spite you. As a creature on the brink of eternity you must give up your mind to the thought of death and judgment and be of a sad countenance every day, but especially on the Lord's day. You must keep the Sabbath very strictly and miserably—you must, in short, be as unlike as possible what you would be if you were not religious, no matter about being merely moral, just, true, generous. You must at least and above all be strict in the keeping of the Sabbath, regular in attending church, pious in the observance of Sacraments and hours of devotion. Are not these the notions of Christianity which are still, I will not say common, for few people entertain the whole of them, but to be found lingering out in many minds—especially some ancient clerical minds—the remainder of a long and prosperous and powerful existence? Judaism over again, Christianity cut in the likeness not of Christ but of Moses, not according to the model of the new Jerusalem in the sermon on the Mount, but to the pattern showed to Moses on Mount Sinai! Human nature and human life are to be subjected to all this harsh and violent treatment, bled and blistered, clipped and tortured out of their original shape, in order to be made Christian and fit for the kingdom of God—with what result history can tell us, and the newspapers, and that critical observation commonly directed to our neighbour which ought to be applied to ourselves.

Properly understood, the religion of Christianity repudiates the ancestry which is thus assigned to it. In regard to harshness and arbitrariness its features are only related by contrast to those of the older religion which it came to supersede. If the Christianity of our age differs from that of many ages preceding ours on the score of being more tolerant, more humane, more rational, the difference up to a certain point would be universally admitted to be in favour of our Christianity. It would be admitted to be a difference in the direction of a return to pure, or, if you choose to call it such, primitive Christianity. There lives not a bigot, possibly even in our country, in which bigotry, like courage and some other virtues, has been a prolific growth ; there lives not a bigot, possibly, who would maintain that the spirit of Christianity was purer, truer, more consistent with itself and with the eternal reality of things, in the hillmen and their persecutors than it is in these times when Christ is preached every way, even in that which is called heresy, without anybody having to go to the stake for it, or to submit to more misunderstanding and misrepresentation than is perhaps common in every sphere of life, including that of keeping a door in the house of God. Up to a certain point it is admitted that the Christianity which is humane, rational, which commends itself to the intelligence and the temper of an enlightened age, is a truer Christianity, nearer the original type than one less humane, less rational, that is to say, more arbitrary, more antagonistic to human nature. Beyond this point the truth may not be so universally admitted, but it is the truth. Pure Christianity is another name, not for what is violently antagonistic to human nature, but for that which finds in human nature itself, as regards every variety of mental, moral and spiritual disability and disorder, the force which is mighty to heal, and bless, and save. As Christianity was at first known in the world, as after a long period of contention, misunderstanding and misrepresentation, it begins to be commonly known again, it distinguishes itself from other religious systems by nothing so much as by the unlimited reliance which it places, not upon authority armed with force or with ferocity to crush resistance, but upon the existence of a better nature within us, kindred to itself and to the skies. The law came by Moses—an external machinery for the production of ecclesiastical piety. Grace and truth, those things which are of inward origin and operation, the healing forces of a better nature, came by Jesus Christ, were quickened in his life and ministry into newness of life and vastness of dominion. I don't find anything said about original sin in the Gospel, as to the amount of depravity, total or otherwise, to be attributed to human nature, not a word, as far as I know, was ever said by our Lord. But whatever may be held to be the Christian view of these matters, it is certain that what according to the doctrine of Christ is held to be wrong in human nature, is not to be put right, according to that doctrine, by any kind of arbitrary compulsion, but simply and solely through the restored and quickened action of that which is spiritual in man; first that which is natural, then that which is spiritual, the one in a sense being as natural as the other. It is the story of physicians and their patients over again, with this difference only, that the true idea of medical treatment would seem to be a discovery of these latter days, whereas with regard to spiritual religion the right method has had almost to be re-discovered some eighteen or nineteen centuries after it had found for itself consummate and world-wide expression. One thing the enlightenment of our age has done for us, it has delivered the immense majority of religious minds from the superstition which made as much account of a text of Scripture, perhaps wrongly translated, as of the spirit of a book, or of all the books put together. We have come to look to the spirit of the writings to which we assign the character of sacred oracles, and in comparison with that to make small account of a verse here and there, with regard to which, perhaps; scholars cannot exactly inform us whether it ought to be there or not. Looking thus to the general scope of the teaching of Christ, we have no difficulty in seeing what religion was meant by Him to be in relation to all moral and spiritual disability and disease. It was not to be a system of bleeding and blistering, of curing by counter-irritation, of making six days of the week holy by making the seventh miserable, of making earth a place of torment in order to render heaven accessible, of overcoming one disease by the production of another. It was to be a kindred influence with the sunshine, and the air of shores and hills, and the kindly ties of home, and the sympathy which is born of comradeship in adversity and sorrow— it was to be an influence kindred with all these in restoring to health those that were ready to perish. Every way you choose to look at it, this is the character of the Christianity of Christ. Its method is not, in the name of the divine, to order human nature to be other than it is, but to be what it is at its best. Christianity, as we in our age begin to understand it and to see its divine perfection, does not seek to terrify us from evil, it is not a revelation of a worse hell than pagans dreamed or Jews imagined, it seeks to win us to good, it is a revelation of the only heaven which has any reality—that to which the good man and true belongs and of which he knows the blessedness and peace, sitting by his fireside and surrounded by his children. To touch and rouse sympathies in us which are the best part of our nature, and which intercourse with our kind has left dormant or dead, it brings us into contact with that Supreme Lover, Benefactor, without whom a sparrow cannot fall to the ground, who numbers the hairs of our heads, who is kind to the evil and unthankful, who will have all men to be saved and to come to the knowledge of the truth. In thus representing the highest of all as the best of all, as perfect eternal goodness and mercy, as not almighty force but boundless pity and mercy and forgiveness, Christianity appeals to human nature as susceptible of being moved by influences divinely sweet and pure and tender, and yet at the same time as native to the better part of man as breathing is to his lungs or sight to his eyes. In the same way, having no code of laws to propound according to which other goodness than natural goodness might be produced, referring to the law of love and sympathy written in the soul itself as supreme and universal; setting aside goodness after any other law than of human nature as no goodness at all; recognising in the good Samaritan though he was a heathen, in the prodigal's father though he is not reported to have been a believer, natural goodness as good, the best of human nature as divine; blessing in the name of God all those persons and all those things that are blessed by honest, good, pure, true hearts the world over; pronouncing that goodness which is natural to be the highest goodness of all—in all this what Christianity does is to adopt the line of the modern physician who, instead of torturing his patient into health or into his grave by arbitrary and violent treatment, submissively seeks to aid nature to do its own wonderful work of restoration and healing. It finds in human nature itself, not in the exercise of any arbitrary exterior pressure or compulsion, the best, and indeed the only, possible resources for the production of that goodness, not churchy but human, which is life eternal and divine.

If this be so, we have reason to be thankful that we live in an age in which, as in the treatment of the body so also in the treatment of the soul, the light no longer shineth in darkness, the darkness comprehending it not. It does not follow, of course, that all who cling to what is old in religion are made worse while those who adopt what is new are made better. We cannot thus distinguish between old-fashioned views of Christianity and those which begin to find general acceptance as more rational and more consistent with the teaching of the life of Christ. No system of treatment of the soul, any more than any particular treatment of disease, is attended with manifest, immediate, invariable success. But if there is to be any treatment of the one or of the other, it is a great matter that it should be right rather than wrong, if it were only because wrong treatment makes things worse than no treatment. And as regards different phases of our faith, it must be said that Christianity was likely to fail of its object, and even to produce evil instead of good, when it pitched its pretensions too high and in an arbitrary manner required from men, from motives little known here below, the virtues of angels. Then it was likely enough to make human nature worse instead of better—not more but less humane. On the other hand, that doctrine seems more likely to have some good result, which lays stress upon the fact that what religion claims as due to God is exactly what reason dictates as best for man, and that whatever may or may not be required of us by men or by churches, what is required of us by the eternal law within us, is to be true to ourselves, to do justly, to love mercy, and to walk humbly with God. In this sense spiritual religion, the religion of Christ which we profess, has a future of which no criterion or prophecy is supplied by the past. What pure Christianity, Christianity in its original spiritual form, can do for the healing of the nations, has not been ascertained or determined by the course of Christian history, long as that course has been. How incomplete is the story of redemption, regeneration, salvation for all mankind, of which the opening page was written in song so long ago. There is nothing in it to show that Christianity is effete, and that when it is old it cannot renew its youth. It is younger and fresher to us, perhaps, than at any time since it had just been born, since it was first heard of in an obscure corner of an empire which derided it, but could not crush it or cope with it. If what has been said has any truth in it, what is peculiar to our age in regard to Christianity is, not that here and there a mind is to be found which is influenced by the religion of the Gospels, in its purest, most spiritual form, but that in that form as contrasted with other less spiritual forms, it has begun to gain acceptance with the mass of men who have any powers of thought, any capacity for distinguishing between what is rational and what is opposed to reason and rejected by conscience.

Converts might be made to any form of Christianity at any time and anywhere, but it is not surprising that it has taken ages and ages to accomplish this end—the turning the minds, not of the few but of the many, to that wisdom of the just which consists in seeing things exactly as they are. It is comparatively easy to convert, in a sense, individuals, even nations, from heathenism, cultured or barbarous, to the Christian faith. It is far more difficult, it requires ages and ages, to change modes of thought which have long been established in the world, which have been transmitted from generation to generation, perhaps in their very make and constitution, bodily and mental—it requires ages and ages to change these, to make that spiritual in them which was earthly and sensual. This is what Christianity has been silently doing these many hundreds of years, while it may often have seemed to be doing little or nothing. It is itself a parable of which the parable of the leaven hid in three measures of meal is a partial glimpse. As the final embodiment and consecration of spiritual religion it almost disappears for ages in that which is alien to itself; but it is working its work secretly, bringing about a revolution in the thought and feeling of mankind in relation to the most important of all objects of thought and feeling—a revolution of which we in our day see signs in the heavens above and in the earth beneath. It was no doubt simply by the force of the appeal which it made to the spiritual nature of man that the Christianity of Christ—of the sermon on the Mount, of the parables, of the Cross,—made its first impression on the world, first established itself among the things that are. But once it was established it associated with itself one way and another an overwhelming concourse of minds unspiritual, minds to which it was more necessary, more comfortable, more convenient, to have a religion of some sort than to be sure of what their religion was. Thus, in contact with unspiritual modes of thought prevalent in the world, incorporated in Christian communities and Christian churches, spiritual religion, as it was heard from the lips of Christ and of apostles, was vulgarized, made commonplace, earthly, sometimes sensual, not a little devilish. To change again those prevailing unspiritual modes of thought by which Christianity was debased and weakened could not be the work of one age. It meant not only a revision of a creed, such as might be made by a committee of divines, it signified the reconstruction of the whole fabric of society, changing fundamentally the entire character, mental, social, moral, of men and nations. We in our time see more of the great work of Christianity accomplished in this way than other generations have seen. To us, therefore, it may seem as if the best proof that Christianity is divine is the fact that it is gifted with the power of being ever young. The future belongs to it more than did the past, and herein it is glad tidings for all mankind. The day has come, not of pure religion being numbered with the things that were, but of its putting forth its real miraculous power for the healing of the nations. When the work is done of which we see a marked, and indeed a wonderful progress in our day, of the religion of the Son of Man uniting men and nations in the recognition of love to God and man as life eternal and divine, of religion being made not a cause of strife and hatred and a marplot of all human joy, but a bond of union among men and nations, a principle of co-operation stronger than any political or social tie, then, though the winter wind will still be cold in northern lands, man's ingratitude, dishonesty, cruelty will be felt to be more cutting than the wintry wind; but better than our years have been will be those that will be seen by our children and our children's children, and peace shall be upon Israel.

V.

TRYING TO DO ONE'S BEST.

"Let us not lose heart in well-doing."—Gal. vi. 9.

IN the progress of society, as the result of the organization of industry advancing step by step, life is changed for the mass of men in two respects. In respect to work, which is a great part of their life, classes and divisions, on the one hand, are multiplied in number; on the other hand, there is greater uniformity, superficial uniformity, introduced into the lives of the members of each class and division. In the manufacture of pins, I suppose, one set of workmen are employed upon heads and another class, or more classes than one, upon points. Rows of houses, undistinguishable from each other except by a number on the door, stretching away from the factory gates, form a town, accommodate a multitude of hands who in the books of the firm employing them are known each by a number. This is one result of advancing civilization, a superficial uniformity in the lives of the great mass of mankind.

There is another and different result, a less superficial one. In regard to doing the best they can or the worst they can in such a state of society as ours, highly organized in point of industry, not so well organized in regard to the higher life of mankind, instead of progressive uniformity among the mass of mankind there is progressive difference and disparity. The corruption of the best is the worst. Advanced civilization has more to show both in the way of the best being made of life and the worst being made of it than barbarism or more imperfect civilizations. In those rows and blocks of houses with which we are familiar in great centres of population, which are undistinguishable save by a number on the door; among those hands known by a number to the firm employing them and paying them wages, there is to be met with perseverance in well-doing on the one hand and there is ingenuity and determination in ill-doing, such, I suppose, as you could not match from the records of more simple and primitive communities.

"Let us not lose heart in well-doing"—perhaps a better equivalent for the apostolic phrase than "Let us not be weary in well-doing"—let us not lose heart, that is to say, in trying the best we can in the face of difficulties and adversities. If we speak of that, our own time and the society of which we are a part will supply us with abundant illustrations of what is meant. Ask what it means, and perhaps some such case as this might present itself to the mind of some one acquainted with the houses and the haunts of the poor in Glasgow. There is a father and two daughters, one of whom is a hand in a factory, and the other a deformed creature who has been confined to bed for some years, and who, as a helpless invalid, demands all the attention and assistance to be got from the one effective member of the domestic firm—in her spare hours, spared from sleep. In circumstances like these it is easier to imagine one losing heart than not losing it. Yet it is under circumstances not very unlike these that hundreds and thousands of people, hands in factories and shipyards, keep on trying to do their best all their lives, and do it, not losing heart in well-doing, in a way which is astonishing.

Trying to do one's best in this way I distinguish, of course, from what is often considered the best one can do—living a decent and orderly life with a view to another world and the rewards and punishments that belong to it. In view of what is usually expected to be the outcome of it, there is not much surprise to be felt if people persevere in a regular course of paying their debts, abstinence from swearing and from drink, and going to church. It is not in this line that the perseverance in well-doing which our time and our society has to show is calculated to strike us as astonishing. It is in that other direction, of facing circumstances with a stout heart, and trying to make the best of them just because it seems the natural thing to do, and therefore the only thing to be done. Your mill-worker—with her drunken father and her hunchback sister on her hands, the great concern of whose existence is that the poor-law inspector should not be allowed to come between her and them—she does not go to her work in February mornings thinking of the splendours of the new Jerusalem—most likely not, at any rate. She anticipates the rising of the sun in her going forth, and comes back wearied at night—wearied but ready to begin her voluntary toil: if she has time to think at all, she only thinks of what she is doing as the thing which it would be shameful on her part not to do. Of this sort of trying to do one's best in the face of adverse circumstances there is, thank God, a great deal in the world—enough to be thought a considerable set-off against all that is of another and opposite sort in the society of which we are a part.

At all times, and now more than ever, most of the heroism of the world is unconscious. The best of it is so. Those moral prodigies who attain heroic proportions and, in consequence, occupy a position in relation to ordinary humanity in which homage is so freely lavished upon them that they cannot but become highly conscious of themselves, are apt, like most modern giants on show, to begin to manifest constitutional debility somewhere or somehow. It is, at any rate, most probably in the ranks of commonplace humanity, after all, that the truest heroism is commonest, as far as that means what it does mostly mean—trying to do the best one can in the face of adverse circumstances.

There is a great deal too little of this in the world. That is true. But the wonderful thing after all is, not that there is so little, but that there is so much. On the whole, as regards those duties, obligations, activities, which, though apparently in themselves trivial or at any rate commonplace, make up the sum of human existence, what is remarkable is not that so few people, but that so many people, keep on in a sort of way trying to do the best they can whatever they may happen to meet with in the shape of difficulty or adversity. At the same time this is just to say in other words that it is not so easy for most people to do this as not to require that it should be premeditated and provided for. It is a large part of mankind for whom the advice must have a good deal of force, "Let us not lose heart in well-doing," a great deal more force than the advice, " Buy in the cheapest market and sell in the dearest." There is more risk of things going wrong with most people in regard to well-doing in general than in regard to going to market.

An acute observer of mankind, who was not a cynical observer either, was accustomed to say that at the age of forty men get tired of being honest. About that time of life, according to his observation, men lose heart in trying to do their best as regards honesty. Be that as it may, not many men, I should say, have lived till forty without having had some such experience as that of which the remark is a more or less grotesque and humorous representation. After forty, I should hope, many men continue to be honest who have been honest before, if only from force of habit—honest even in trades and callings and occupations the most open to suspicion on the score of harbouring doubtful characters. It is a calumny, no doubt, to say that no old politician, parliamentary or ecclesiastical, is honest. Neither Jew nor Gentile who on account of age is obliged to wear a peruke is, I suppose, by the same fatality compelled to wear a mask. It is just as certain, however, on the other hand, that in trying to do the best they can as regards honesty among other things, a common experience of mankind is of difficulty and obstruction which does not always diminish, but often increases, with age or with the result of age in an enlarged acquaintance with the world and its ways.

Take as an example of those things as to which the difficulty of keeping on doing one's best is felt often to increase instead of diminish after forty—take as an example, not any disclosure of the bankruptcy court, but that in which there is so much bankruptcy, so much paying sixpence in the pound or nothing at all—I mean friendship. A man goes on, let us suppose, till he is forty trying to do his best not only for his own satisfaction and well-being, but for the comfort and happiness of a circle of friends and acquaintances, including, of course, relatives. If you look into it, that means a great deal. It means the regulation of life in various relations and in a vast variety of circumstances and incidents, not perhaps by the highest standard conceivable, but at any rate by one which is very far from being the lowest, and is very different indeed from no regulation at all. But one event happeneth to all —his wife, or his son, or his daughter dies, or is lost to him in one of those other ways in comparison with which the way of death is that of pleasantness and peace. It is all very well, is it not, in such circumstances to say, Never mind, do not lose heart, bate not a jot of heart or hope, go on exactly as if nothing had happened, persevere in all that welldoing in which your perseverance has been all that your friends could have desired. If the man to whom you say that answers you with a sickly smile which tells that he does not for the present feel quite equal to the effort, what can you say to him or think of him?

Worse than this may happen to a man, of course, in the way of friendship. Friendship is a great part of life, and the best part of it. In trying to do the best we can to cultivate friendship, it is not easy always to distinguish between selfish and unselfish feelings, between what we are doing for ourselves and what we are doing for others. Nor is it needful to distinguish very precisely. It is worth doing the best we can to cultivate friendship, whether it be considered for our own private interest or as a contribution to the wellbeing of society. Is it an experience at all rare with men of forty, or men above forty, that, in proportion as we come to feel more and more the need of friendship as a solace and support amid the cares and troubles of life, we find that there is less of it on which we can thoroughly depend. The worst of this is not that old friendships are reduced in number by the accidents of life and the probability, which is a certainty, of death. Nor is the worst of it perhaps that here and there an old friend, on whom it was thought reliance could be placed in a time of need, is discovered to be unreliable. Worse than all this is the discovery, which perhaps is sometimes unavoidable in the course of a long life with regard to a large circle of friends and acquaintances, that it hardly ever contained an individual altogether worthy of the attachment and affection to which it was once thought he was entitled. When one is urged to do one's best in the way of friendship, this, to say the least, is a discouraging sort of experience—one the effect of which can be recognised sometimes in the advice of ancient sages among us moderns, retired and superannuated Poloniuses, who counsel young men to have few friends, and not to expect much from any of them.

Widen the bounds of life so as to include a larger section of society than a circle of private friends and acquaintances, and possibly, indeed certainly, you widen and deepen this sort of experience. It is in trying to do the best we can at the bidding of social impulse, feeling that it is possible to have and to enjoy life at its widest, best, noblest, intensest—it is just in that direction that we are most certain to meet with difficulties and reverses which put a strain upon the most determined purpose, and try the courage of the stoutest heart. Here, as we cannot but soon discover, the difficulty is that we have to deal not merely with the folly and perversity and wickedness of mankind, more or less remediable, but what is worse, that we have to deal with incorrigible ignorance, and worse still, with the hopeless stupidity, imbecility, and fatuity of a great part of the human race. You might struggle to get the better of the depravity, but what are you to make of the stupidity? No perseverance of yours can touch that. With regard to doing the best we can in the way of doing good to others, it often seems as if we had to fight against nature itself, against the inevitable course of things—a hopeless enterprise altogether. In trying to do our best in this way we seem to be often in no very different position from that of a builder or railway contractor undertaking by means of his best plant to reconstruct and rearrange some part of the solar system.

Our social and religious efforts to improve and elevate the whole community, or some considerable part of it, do not fail altogether, but in what case do they answer sanguine expectations? Our intention in giving our old acquaintance, now in reduced circumstances, a half-crown or a cast-off coat is to help him to regain a position of comfort and respectability from which he has fallen by his misconduct; once more in that way we try to do the best we can for him. Across the street are the pawnshop and the public-house, which receive him and the like of him into what are almost everlasting habitations, and what they make nearly as certain as the alternation of day and night is that the best we can do in this instance should end in failure and something worse. There is a chance of losing heart in trying to do one's best in this way—I mean that of simple benevolence. What is done to be sure does not always fail, but it fails so often that the chance of losing heart in the business is considerable. After all, however, simple benevolence, though a noble department of human life, is a very small, limited department of it. If in that department there is a chance of losing heart in the endeavour always to do the best we can, in many or most other departments of human existence, a great part of mankind give up trying altogether. In much the larger part of our existence, as in the matter of friendship, we are actuated partly by regard for our own interests, which may be called selfishness, partly by social instincts, impulses, sympathies, which are more or less unselfish. In this wide sphere of activity, at any rate when the width of it is recognised, to keep on trying to do the best we can in the face of such difficulties as we are certain to encounter, requires determination and perseverance possessed only by the few. The order of the day here is not, You may chance, unless you take care, to lose heart; it is rather, Give it up altogether, for it is impracticable. For it is here, above all, that you find you have usually to deal not only with the perversity and folly of the greater part of mankind, but with what is, as I have said, so much more intractable— stupidity, blindness, and imbecility. Thus it is as if the difficulties of the Irish question seem rather to multiply than to diminish when one or two attempts have been made to settle it. Give it up, is the word which occurs to many or most people on both sides of politics. There is no use trying to settle it. Do you not see that the difficulties are only increasing; do you not see what sort of people you have to deal with in trying to settle it? Anyone who takes an active part in political life or in public affairs of any description must lay his account with often having more experience of annoyance and vexation than of satisfaction and enjoyment. It may be true that some portion of the nation or of the community must occupy themselves with these matters—that this is essential to the well-being and progress of all human society; but what many people say to themselves and to their friends is, You see what is to be got by meddling with affairs of the sort. Settle the question as to doing the best you can in regard to them by doing nothing at all.

So in regard to domestic life, the training of children, perhaps, or the treatment of domestics, what trying to do one's best means is incessant thought and worry and anxiety, with what result? Why, perhaps that children who are very carefully brought up don't turn out better than children who are less carefully reared, and that servants who are treated with exceptional kindness and consideration, don't see it and look out for another situation. Give it up altogether, is therefore what many people are disposed to say in matters of this sort after a short experience of trying to do the best they can.

There is the same story to be told in regard to industrial and commercial life. It may be all very true to say that honesty is the best policy, but in practice that does not mean that the honest man is sure always to be the most successful man. In all trades and professions and callings, I suppose, there are successful quacks, impostors, adventurers. To be thoroughly honest often means to compete with this class of men for success and to be beaten by them, not because they deserve to win, but because so large a part of the public are stupid enough to be imposed upon by their artifices and pretences. Give up trying to do the best you can; it does not pay; follow some less stringent rule. You have a good cause to maintain or to promote, and you are so certain that it is good that you are willing to take some trouble about it. How much trouble are you willing to take? is the question you will most likely have to answer before long. It is a good thing to stand up for truth, fair-play, justice, kindness and fellow-feeling between man and man, and everybody, or almost everybody, feels that it is good. But other people don't see what you see. Their ignorance, prejudice, mental feebleness and blindness is such that you can make no impression upon them as to the truth of your views and the sincerity and rectitude of your feelings. You are willing to take some trouble to have these matters ruled as you would like to see them ruled. The question comes to be, How much trouble are you willing to take? It is not perhaps, Will you go to the stake, if need be? but, Will you live most of your life in hot water? When that is the question in regard to trying to do the best we can, give it up altogether is the conclusion to which many people are apt to come, not perhaps all at once, but gradually and with certainty.

"He that will speak the truth must expect martyrdom on both sides," was said in times different from ours, when Whig and Tory, Churchman and Nonconformist, rationalist and orthodox believer, fought with other weapons than those with which they encounter each other now. But it is still true. All mankind feel that it is a great thing, manly and noble on the one hand, of priceless advantage to society and to human progress on the other hand, to search honestly for truth, and when you have found it to utter it fearlessly. Everybody agrees with everybody about that. But is there any walk of life in which a man can devote himself to the search for truth and to speaking the truth which he has found in a fearless fashion, without discovering for himself that it is not usually the way to success in life but the straight road in the opposite direction? He has, perhaps, some reward in the approbation of the few, but it is a hundred to one that he forfeits the favour of the many, which means so much in the way of bread and butter as well as renown. Those who know better than he how to address themselves to the prejudice, stupidity, cupidity of the multitude, leave him behind not only in the race for riches, but in the competition for credit and reputation. In trying to do one's best in this department of human affairs the chance of losing heart sometimes is, for most men, not so much a chance as a certainty.

Well, then, as all this may be taken to show, it seems as if much of our trying the best we can were fighting, as I have said, against the course of nature itself, so much of it having thus to be opposed to the intractable ignorance and stupidity, and not merely the folly and perversity, of our fellow-men. It is all owing to the landlords having been allowed to appropriate the soil, says one authority, that so much is wrong, that there is so much to put right, that well-doing is so manifold and so difficult a business, under the conditions of the most advanced and civilized society. It is all owing to what took place in that happy garden in which the tenant and the proprietor were one, says another. The truth of the matter seems to be that the development of mankind has been and will continue to be a slow process, and is necessarily characterized by much inequality in the condition of nations, classes, individuals. The same position of advancement is not reached at one and the same time by every member of a community. Enlightenment is the portion of the few. Comparative ignorance and degradation is the lot of the many. In trying to do the best we can according to any rational view of life and its possibilities, we share the enlightenment of the few. That is one advantage. One disadvantage and disability is that we have to contend in a great part of our activity with the comparative ignorance, unreason, mental and moral feebleness and blindness of the many, and with the degradation which results from it. That disadvantage and disability cannot be altered in a day or in a generation to the extent to which we should like to see it altered. To this extent, but only to this extent, is it true that in trying to do the best we can according to the best we know, we fight against the course of nature and are engaged in a hopeless enterprise.

It is just because there is progress, development in human life and human society, that there is inequality and disparity in it, such as makes it so difficult, in our social relations particularly, to keep on trying to do our best instead of adopting some less stringent rule of action. If there were no development there would be no such inequality as there is between the best of men and the worst, and no such difficulty as there is for most men not to lose heart in trying to do the best they can.

There is, then, a conclusion to which all this brings us; I shall have to state it rather than prove it or illustrate it. It is because in trying to do the best we can, it often seems, as regards direct and immediate effects and with reference only to a limited period of time and a limited portion of human society, as if we were contending against nature itself, that we are so apt to lose heart in well-doing. To prevent this consequence of taking a narrow view of things, the best that can be done is to take a wider view, viz., that development, progress, is the law of human life and society, though the process may seem to be, and in point of fact is, slow and unequal. In trying to do the best we can, in never losing heart in the business, we are partners with the Eternal in accelerating that process, however it may seem that our effort and endeavour is for the time unavailing and abortive. However it may seem to be fighting against nature and the course of things, it is in reality, and in a wider view, working out the Eternal order, to keep on trying to do our best in the face of all difficulties and reverses. That is a view of things to the truth of which history is a witness. There is progress, though it is slow. To take that view, and to give it the place which it ought to hold in all our thoughts, is the best provision that can be made by us against the great calamity of losing heart in well-doing.

God said to man when he made him, at any rate the moment he sprang into conscious existence, Do thy best, Winter and Summer, in plenty, in poverty, with circumstances to favour or to withstand, and thou shalt live. Though it is not recorded in the Bible, I know that it is so, because it is so written in the very nature of man. Do thy best, never lose heart in doing that, and thou shalt live. Other life worth the name than trying to do the best he can, there is not for man upon the earth or anywhere else.

To reinforce this one great consideration as to not losing heart in well-doing, there is another—that to which I have referred—that this perseverance is required in the interests of the race, as much as for the well-being of the individual. And on this ground of the well-being of mankind, the appeal in favour of well-doing on the part of the individual can be made with effect, if it is rightly made, to all mankind. If it appeals to little or no feeling on our part to be told that we can only make the best of life for ourselves by trying to do the best we can, it may yet appeal to some feeling in us to be made to see that in that way we do something for our kind which we are not at liberty in their interest to do or not to do, but which we are bound to do as much as we are bound to continue in existence. If there is not some such feeling in us, to which this consideration can appeal with effect, it can only be said, not that we are not ready to die, but that we are not fit to live—that from our composition the best part of human nature has been somehow omitted or abstracted.

We owe to our kind more than we can repay by never losing heart in well-doing, by trying to do the best we can in the face of all difficulties and reverses. That is one consideration which presents itself in connection with this view of human society as one whole. Any advantage which we have, social, intellectual, moral, spiritual, over any of our fellow-men, and which, by dividing or seeming to divide us from them and our interests from theirs, makes it the more difficult for us to do the best we can for ourselves and for them—any advantage of this sort we owe a great deal less to any meritorious effort of our own than to what has been done for us in the course of that progress of the race to which so many generations have contributed their share. If there is an aristocracy of intellect and virtue in existence, if there is a spiritual aristocracy, it rests upon the basis of a vast democracy more ancient and for the most part more worshipful and venerable than itself. This was not the view, I know, of an eminent man who was asked at a parliamentary investigation what education he would give the mass of the community. He said he would give them religious education. When he was asked further how they could be educated religiously without having other education, his reply was—" Suffering—whom the Lord loveth he chasteneth." His notion was that the aristocracy of virtue and knowledge is self-supporting; and that, that being the case, the democracy, whatever it is, may be left to shift for itself except when, as a last shift, it appeals to heaven. And this is a view of things which is not altogether antiquated. But it is exactly, I need not say, the opposite of the truth. No man is in a high or a good position in this world in regard to the higher interests of mankind who does not owe his advantages so much to his kind rather than to himself, that in trying to do the best he can for others he is doing no more than repaying some part of his debt.

There is progress, though it be slow and unequal. That, let me say in conclusion, is the great truth which we have to keep in mind so as not to lose heart in well-doing. It is because, among unnumbered generations of men, countless individuals have lived by the rule of trying to do their best in spite of difficulties and reverses, that we are where we are to-day with our hopes of to-morrow and of heaven. Perhaps it is always the few who live by that rule in anything like perfect and saintly obedience. But let as many as do live by it give up the effort to live by it, and the consequence must be not merely that we and they should no further advance in civilization or in moral and spiritual refinement, but that we and they should retrograde into barbarism. Let us not lose heart in well-doing, for in due season we shall reap if we faint not. It is a contribution which we are bound to make to the well-being and progress of mankind, and in making which it cannot but be that we shall enjoy in the course of life and in all its changes the best and highest satisfaction that the soul of man can have, in feeling that there is an eternal order, and that it is just and good, and that in submitting to it we are at one with that Father and Friend of all that lives, who is the beginning and the end of all things. The spirit, if not the letter, of the whole teaching of Christ is represented in saying, Do thy best and thou shalt live. His appeal is constantly to the natural instincts of mankind—those which are concerned in well-doing, not in the narrow sense of religion being a part of life, but in the sense of life being all of the nature of religion. What is dictated to us by nature or by our position in human society as to doing the best we can, nothing less, if nothing more, *that* he takes and places in the light of the Eternal and Divine—*that* it is his whole doctrine to say, is what is pleasing to God, *that* is salvation and eternal life. In the doing of it a man becomes a son of God, and to him the kingdom of heaven is already open.

VI.

THE RIGHT OF THE POOR.

"Call the poor and the maimed."—LUKE xiv. 13.

BAD as it is to have a low or unworthy aim in life, it is still worse to have none at all. It is so because, in the pursuit of low or at least unworthy aims, many men exercise and cultivate fine and almost noble qualities of character, and certainly live lives which are in a measure satisfactory to themselves and useful to society; whereas the man who is without a definite aim, besides being very much at the mercy of all influences hostile to a good life, has many chances to one against his life turning out either satisfactory to himself or useful to others. Perhaps the lives which might be described as aimless are the majority of those with which we have much acquaintance or familiarity. They drift along to one consummation or another, rather than push forward to a goal the attainment of which is the fulfilment of high hope and the accomplishment of a great purpose. Just the very last thing in the world which is to be assumed, however, as probable with regard to this fact is, that it is the occasion of any deep and lasting regret. Such regret is perhaps rare enough to remind those who have read it, of the prologue to one of the greatest of modern tragedies. In that prologue the question between the manager of the theatre, who wants a new piece for his stage; the poet, who is expected to supply him with what he wants; and the actor—the critic off the boards, who plays the part of literary adviser—the question between these three is what sort of piece it would be best to attempt. In this colloquy it is the poet's part to insist upon those lofty views of the end and aim of poetry which almost identify it with revelation and religion—represent it, therefore, as possibly in some cases appealing rather to posterity for a just appreciation of its merits than to the undiscerning public of to-day. To his coadjutors nothing could be more foreign or fantastic than such notions. One after the manner of his kind insists that the success of an entertainment in which poetry is concerned is to be measured by the entertainment which it gives, not to posterity, but to the living world; the other characteristically preaches that that success is to be estimated by results which can be expressed in pounds, shillings, and pence. It comes in the way of this latter personage's argument to characterize the various sorts of people for whose entertainment something new and memorable is to be provided, to throw off in rough-and-ready outline a sketch of society as it is, of the social organization in which the dramatic poet and performer among others have to play their parts. Here are the victims of weariness and dulness, there of gluttony or drink or passion — people whose thoughts, even in the theatre, are of further excitement and dissipation. It is for such people as these that his poet has to work, and the work should be suited to *their* tastes, not to *his* fantastic humours. What do these people care for his divine raptures and ecstasies and heroics in regard to the majesty and beauty of nature, or the wonders and glories of man's world of thought and feeling, or art for art's sake, or love, the crown and flower of life? Not a straw; nothing of the sort will tell upon the cash box, except to keep it hollow. The ideal, in all its forms, is the poetry of life. This, or something like this, is the relation in which it stands to the multitude and the multitude to it. It presents itself for the most part to minds pre-occupied, this with business, that with pleasure— so pre-occupied that it has but little chance of making much impression on them. Hence regret as to unfulfilled ideals is rather a feeling widely diffused than keenly experienced. It would be for most men to forsake their own familiar prosaic world and to follow the poet into his world of moonshine to have a divine discontent with themselves as to not making the best of existence. They have no time and no heart for poetry like this. Their hearts are engrossed with their business or their amusements, their pleasures, their ambitions. Talk to them of higher aims, and practically what they have to say is: "Call again." All this may be true, however, and yet it may be the case that there are few minds, and these comparatively aimless minds, that are not visited occasionally with compunctions and regrets which, if I may so express myself, have reference to an ideal life of some sort, of the attractions of which they are in a measure conscious—to purposes and intentions, hopes and aspirations, once entertained, but never fulfilled. As much of this feeling as does exist—of regret, I mean, having reference to some more or less noble ideal of life—may be accounted for best of all, perhaps, in one way. Just as the mind's demand for unity in its own operations and results is only satisfied when the ideas concerned in the explanation of the phenomena of the universe are reduced to simplicity which admits of no further simplification; so, as regards the whole world of human thought, that demand is satisfied only when it is shown how all the complex and varied forms and processes of intellect and feeling can be traced to their origin in impressions and ideas so elementary that no explanation of them can be given. It is from this point of view that we are now accustomed to trace the progress of mind, and of civilization which is the outward expression of that progress. That view of life on this globe which is steadily displacing, by the cumulative weight of evidence in its favour, every other view—that view which connects together the sublimest efforts of reason on the part of mankind with the earliest and simplest forms of existence and intelligence—opens in the dim past of history, and beyond history, a field for the exercise of thought in regard to what mind is and how it has grown, the extent and interest of which are simply inexpressible. Ask, in this point of view, what has been the origin of this or that institution or custom or sentiment or law or mode of thought or expression. Before the last word can be said to have been spoken on that subject, most likely you have to be taken back over the whole field of history, and even beyond history to much that is only matter of inference or conjecture. Be the theory of evolution true or not, as far as the origin of man is concerned, it is beyond doubt that all that is great and far-reaching in our modern thought, whether in one department of things or another, has been won for thought in the course of unnumbered ages, and that the first beginnings in the mighty conquest have been made by men whose intelligence seems nearer akin to the highest intelligence of the inferior orders of creation than to that of the loftiest intellects of modern times. In every department of human thought what a history of struggle and failure is brought before us by the growth of human intelligence, culture, civilization. All those modes of thought with which we are so familiar as to have the feeling that they must have been born with us, have, in point of fact, had a history going back into the night of ages—a history of intelligence not much beyond that of the inferior orders of creation, waxing through infinite struggle and difficulty to that form and stature in which it feels itself to be kindred to the divine. Thoughts and feelings in which the governing forces of our lives, as far as they have any consistency, reside, are in this point of view an inheritance from ages of which the explanation is to be sought where no records ever existed. So it is that in the history of thought, thus conceived of, that which strikes us as most notable is the struggle and difficulty with which thought has freed itself from error and illusion, noxious to human life, obstructive to the progress of human society. What enormous, what terrible systems of error and iniquity have everywhere reared themselves in this world—reared themselves with infinite toil—only to be again with infinite difficulty overturned and removed. Yet it has all been in the natural course of things.

Now that which on the scale of history is so strange and perplexing, and withal so grand a spectacle—this struggle and conflict belonging to the growing intelligence of the race, most of it gigantic failure—is repeated and reflected in the experience of every generation and of every individual. The problems and enigmas of life, as well as some of those belonging to learned and scientific research, are as hard to solve as ever, and the conditions under which they have to be solved in the brief space of time allotted to man upon the earth are in many respects not different now from what they were in the ages before history. On this globe at the present moment, much as has been won for thought by the struggles and endeavours of the race, there are portions of mankind in whose condition there is exactly reproduced and represented every phase of the long conflict from its very commencement. So in every civilized society like our own we have its different stages all represented in the actual intelligence and character of whole classes and certainly of individuals belonging to different classes. If you put aside names and attend to things in the case of these classes or individuals, you can see that their intelligence and culture stand much where they stood when the human mind was with infinite difficulty and struggle emancipating itself from errors, illusions, superstitions, iniquities of which the names are now forgotten. So unequally, that is to say, for one reason or another, is the whole stock of intelligence gained by mankind, distributed even in civilized society, that if you but choose to look for the mind of any distant century or alien race in your own time, among your own contemporaries, you will find it there to the very life, ready to sit for its portrait.

I take this view of the origin, progress, and distribution of intelligence to account for the feeling being so widely diffused as it is that life is a failure, that it has fallen behind its own ideal. Owing to the stock of intelligence and culture being increased, and preserved from age to age, the ideal view of life of the best minds of one generation is preserved for another—preserved so as to have some influence not only on the best minds of that age but upon minds of every order. So, also, all that relates to an ideal of human life in the best minds of any generation has for inferior minds a certain royalty and majesty of its own to which tribute and deference have to be paid. Ideas and sentiments belonging to a high ideal of life, which the best minds of our age have received by inheritance from the best of another age and to which they have added something of their own—such ideas and sentiments reach other minds not at all prepared to entertain and realize them. So there is mingled, to a certain extent, in the experience of one and the same individual the experience of different ages of the history of the world. Something belongs to the time that now is, a great deal to other times. Ideas and sentiments which human society in its highest circles of intelligence has left far behind it in its lowest circles it still retains. Many ingenious minds have exercised themselves in bringing to light in the lives and character of living men and women what survives in them of some past phase of the history of thought. They have shown us old foes and old friends, good and bad causes, wearing new faces among our contemporaries. That which has been thus done by clever novelists and learned historians, partially, and for their own particular purpose, may be done by almost anybody who has any powers of observation, on a large scale and with a striking effect. Just those ideas, sentiments, passions which we now see operative and predominant in the lives and characters of multitudes of men, in business, in love, in politics, in social life, are, thinly veiled, the same as in other ages, possibly what we now call the dark ages, held undisputed possession of the human mind. The only difference is that these ideas and sentiments, all connected once with a certain universally accepted ideal of life, have now to accommodate themselves to the different ideal which is entertained by the best minds of the present time. It might not, perhaps, be charitable to say it in presence of many people to whom the remark applies, but it is true beyond doubt, that in almost every circle of society at the present day, highly civilized as society may be said to be, it is possible to recognise types of character and life all the ideas and sentiments of which belong to ages before the birth of Christ, or to the dark ages since—types perfectly pure and unmistakable, though in some slight and superficial degree affected by the influences of modern culture. This is the case, I cannot help thinking, with regard to no small part of what is called fashionable or respectable society. It is shown to be the case by such facts as that still in these sections of society, rank and wealth are of more account than worth or genius. A single fact of this kind will be found to signify, if it is only carefully examined, that whatever thin veneer of Christian or other culture is commonly applied to character in these sections of society, generally speaking the ideas and sentiments, the aims and aspirations which go to form character are those which belong to the age in which might was right, in which it was the rule

> " That they should take who have the power,
> And they should keep who can ; "

in which, too, it was well believed by both parties that "only the brave"—or, as we should say, the ambitious and fortunate—"deserve the fair." In this point of view it is impossible not to recognise something grotesque in the connection between the newest and freshest life of the time and life older than the garden of Eden; as, for example, in so many of the youths of the present generation who, unfurnished with ideas, or possibly with brains into which ideas could be put, knowing nothing of themselves or of the world but that they have desires and passions to be gratified, and that the world has pleasures to offer at certain fixed prices, set up for being gentlemen, and expect us to recognise in them, not the original barbarian, from whom possibly the best of us are descended, but the very beau-ideal of humanity.

Consider in this view the growth and progress of mind, the co-existence in it of the thought, the ideas and sentiments of all ages, and you have the key to much of the life of the time as it is characterized more or less by a sense of failure and disappointment. Some glimpses of the better and nobler ends of human existenee, some ideas, sentiments, aspirations, belonging to a lofty ideal of life, are the capital—the intellectual capital— with which many of us set out in life. It is our inheritance from all the ages that have been, or a gift to us from the best minds still devoted to the life of thought. How soon this capital can be expended every one knows by his own experience, or by attending to the observations of others. In the susceptible period of youth it is sufficient to keep life up to a certain height of hope and aspiration. It is the young man's dream, perhaps his pious resolution, that no vulgar, common-place, or sordid existence shall be his, but one, in this respect or that, at least something higher, greater, nobler than the life of the crowd. But the ardour of youth once checked and moderated by experience of the difficulties and obstructions in any career but that which is customary and commonplace, perhaps a trifle sordid and crooked, what follows in most cases is, that just the ideas and sentiments that prevail in the life of the crowd are those that assert themselves more and more. What comes after is a struggling, harassed, baffled existence, not that of a hero or a saint but of a common-place man; and so the lofty ideal is set aside, to be remembered only on occasions, and then, of course, with a shudder or a sigh. It is not the life which we once intended to live, it is not the goal we meant to reach, most of us, I suppose, who have lived at all, are disposed to say—not without some heartache which belongs to that reflection. By the light which is in us, and which cannot be altogether extinguished, a shadow of ourselves is thus thrown before us across the world of human life, the effect of which is to involve the whole life of man to our minds in that deepest and dreariest of the shades of night which we call vanity.

The same experience belongs, in a different form, to that part which we have in the life of the community and of the race. Utopias grow more ridiculous every age, millenniums are farther off every hundred and every thousand years. In every department of things in which the activity, energy, enthusiasm of the reformer is called forth, his hopes, for the most part, are like to be betrayed. All abuses die hard, and in dying leave their offspring well endowed. It is, every other day or year, as if that new era which is the oldest of men's dreams—the era of peace, happiness, freedom, enjoyment for the million—had commenced in the new invention, or the new movement, or the new franchise, or the new society, or the new Ministry of all the talents or all the virtues, or in the last stage of the progress from monarchy to democracy. But immediately, again, it is always as if the new era would never come. Every Act of Parliament begins with a "whereas," which is usually followed by a statement of the necessity for the repeal of some other statute or series of statutes, this again to be repealed in due time with another whereas, and so on indefinitely, as if to have it shown in the statute book, as nowhere else, that all legislation is abortive, in the sense of being good only for the temporary redress of evils which cannot be abolished. These hopes appertaining to the life of the society of which we are a part we share in proportion to the activity of our minds and the force of our sympathies. The disappointment, the continual disappointment of them, is what we have to share in the same way. The result to many whose feelings are perhaps stronger than their judgment, is that they settle down into a comfortable or a grim determination to despair of the progress of mankind, and to hold their sympathies aloof from the struggling life in which they have part. A juster view of things, however, and one which does less violence to the best instincts of the human heart, is that which is suggested by the considerations to which I have referred touching the unequal distribution in civilized society of the hardly acquired store of culture and intelligence. Every civilization is compounded of all civilizations, and of barbarisms lingering out a decayed existence into the bargain. Every religion, in its actual institutions and potentialities, is a medley of all religions, including fetishism, serpent-worship, mammon-worship, devil-worship, the worship of the golden calf, and I know not what besides. In every community, in its various grades, well marked in some, more indistinct in others, there is to be traced every phase through which social life has passed in all the ages, even the darkest of the dark, the rudest of the rude, the vilest of the vile. This is the explanation of the fact that the new era is so long in coming, that the millennium recedes as mankind advances, that Utopias vanish into space, and that in every soul of man in which there is the love of mankind, hope is kindred to despair or sick unto death. That which commends itself to the best thought of the best minds as the thing to be done for the welfare and advancement of the community is the very thing, perhaps the only thing, that can be done or proposed; but nevertheless we may look for its miscarrying after all, just because, in order that it should succeed, what is required is that the best thought of the best minds should be diffused as it is not yet, nor shall be for generations. Do not expect wonders from that project and this reform, which would work wonders if your civilization or your religion were all of one piece, since it has to work—if at all—among civilizations and religions as distinct from each other, though combined in your social life, as any that are separated from each other by thousands of years or of miles.

Specially let me note, in a single word in conclusion, how it stands with the supreme ideal, which we call the Christian religion. The ideal of human society which is expressed in saying "Thy kingdom come" belongs to a system of thought than which it is impossible there should ever exist anything more sublime or more divine— that of all men living as if in constant recognition of the fact that duty to man is duty to God. It is an ideal which presupposes, for its fulfilment, the fulfilment of all other ideals that have ever in the history of thought presented themselves to the human mind. As to that ideal there is not a mind in any civilized community so dull as not to see that the likelihood of its being fulfilled is the likelihood that the millennium, which has been receding for some ages, will change its course and make swift progress hitherwards, nobody knows how. Dreadful to think of, is it not, dreadful because true, here in this island this ideal has been in view of the multitude for ages, as the brazen serpent was in the view of the Jews in the wilderness, and still it is a question with us whether we should not empty our jails and erase from the face of the earth half the dwellings of men in our cities, before we talk any more of sending missionaries to Africa or the South Sea Islands. There are three thousand languages in existence, so I believe, in every one of which the name of Christ is named. It is not without a meaning in regard to his followers that he came not to send peace on earth but a sword. When is the Christian era going to begin, is still the question of almost every thoughtful Christian at present breathing the breath of life. There is an ideal the grandest of all, with regard to which the feeling of mankind is—alas that it should be so much a dream!—a dream never to be fulfilled. So where there is Christian thought and Christian life, and where there is none, or none that knows itself to be Christian, there is in regard to religion, as in regard to other things, sadness, disappointment, despair of the progress of mankind. The view of things which I have suggested, however, gives us a more hopeful and cheerful anticipation. In its purest and loftiest forms the

Christian ideal of life is part of a system of thought the rest of which belongs, not to any or every civilization, but to one alone, the highest of all; certainly not to every one of those civilizations, even the lowest and vilest, which ours includes. You are preaching your gospel at present, as far as the bulk of your community is concerned, not to the Jew or the Greek, but to the barbarian whose tongue you know not and who knows not yours. Your ideal belongs to this time and to the highest conceivable civilization. All the ideas and sentiments and aims of the multitude of minds to whom you present it belong to other times and other civilizations—for the most part actually the most ancient times and the very lowest civilizations. No wonder if in Protestant countries with reference to the results of this incongruity there should be whispers like this—" Were it not better if we went back to the dark ages for a more effective Christian ideal than the one we have: is it safe after all to shut up the devil and to do away with eternal punishment?" So there is regret which is wide— if not always deep—regret as to the life of man, as far as all its ideals are concerned, being but vanity and vexation of spirit. My aim has been to suggest—it could only be in a fragmentary and desultory fashion—what is the origin and, therefore, what is the meaning of this regret, so widely and so variously felt in every generation. The idea that the origin of it all is the perversity, the incurable perversity, of human nature, is one that cannot be entertained without loss and damage to all good hearts and all good causes. It dictates letting things alone in this world till they mend of themselves; to which there should be added for the sake of clearness—" and that will be never." So, too, in regard to our individual lives and any hopes and aspirations which still belong to them, it bids us make little effort since much is sure to be abortive. I suggest, I think, a truer and at the same time a more wholesome view when I say that it is not the perversity of human nature, but the slow and unequal growth and distribution of human intelligence, which is to be taken as accounting for the hope deferred of mankind in regard to all their loftiest ideals. We would have religion first, grace first, heaven upon earth first, the millennium first. This is not God's way. He will, it appears, have education first, that education of which the history begins beyond all history in the night of ages, and to which in the case of millions of the human race there still belong the confusions and darkness of chaos and old night. In this view the millennium, far off as it may be, is not too far off to be to a lover of his kind a goal to be reached in the attainment of which some effort should be spent. In this view of things, all that we are or have that is truly human or divine is not our own; we owe it to the race to which we belong. "We are members one of another," and only pay our just and lawful debt to humanity when our lives are devoted to the advancement of our kind. In this view of things, the duty of forgiving till seventy times seven the faults, the follies, the sins and crimes of our fellow-creatures, is the duty of remembering that they are our own poorer brethren, poorer and needier in respect of all that makes life worth having, and that their share of the great inheritance of the race has been less than ours. In this view of things, what we have to say to ourselves in regard to our unfulfilled aims and aspirations and hopes—all the best and worthiest of them at least—is not, "It is useless to think of them, better to forget them and leave them behind us;" but rather this, "They are our inheritance from ages unnumbered, in which men sought with infinite toil and effort to rise in the scale of being, not above their nature, but according to their nature—they are the final result of experience which has been won at unspeakable cost, and they point us to the true ends and aims of life, if life is to be worth anything." They are not visionary but real, none the less that they cannot be fulfilled. Our one chance, if all experience of mankind that is worthy of remembrance and of honour is to be trusted—our one chance of good in this life or in any life, is to bring as far as may be all our thoughts and all our life, yet unordered and confused with regard to these ideals, into harmony with them. So near the end of this year as we are, these reflections, as far as they have any weight at all, will be thought to have a special weight. To-day, appropriately enough, we make our annual collection for the hospitals of the city. With regard to these and similar institutions, the necessity for the existence of which is the existence in sin and misery of so large a part of the community—with regard to these institutions, any difficulty which is felt as to obtaining for them adequate support is due above all, I think, to the feeling that in most cases in which they have relief to offer to the miserable, it is to the miserable whose misery is of their own creation. Practically they are institutions maintained by the rich for the benefit of the poor. It is the feeling among the rich that the poor have mostly their own habits to blame for their misfortunes and calamities, which checks the flow of sympathy and of money towards these institutions. In that view of things on which I have insisted this morning, you see how mistaken a feeling this is. The truth with regard to those classes for whose benefits our charitable institutions are maintained is not so much that they are degraded as that they have not yet had a chance to rise. It has not yet come to their turn to be what we are in point of civilization, culture, all that is excellent and estimable or wonderful for which we give ourselves credit. We have great sympathy— some of us—for the negro because he is a negro, therefore a heathen, a barbarian, perhaps a cannibal. For the victims of a civilization the greater part of which is near akin to barbarism, let us have at least as much sympathy as we have for the black man.

VII.

CONSIDER THE LILIES.

"Consider the lilies of the field how they grow."—Matt. vi. 28.

EVERY gospel that is preached under the sun is at once old and new. Every form in which the religious instinct finds expression for itself, along with something that belongs to time and place, has in it much more of human nature as old as Adam. Every scribe that is instructed into the kingdom of heaven brings forth out of his treasures things new and old, and it is to be reminded of this to remark that the gospel which is preached by John Ruskin and other devout Christians of the present day, that gospel in which there is so much discourse of the beautiful, is in substance as well as largely in form the very gospel which was preached by Plato four hundred years before Christ. The thoughts of men are widened by the process of the suns, the human mind is not constitutionally altered or amended. If after a long period of neglect the gospel which was much preached by Plato, of the close connection between the beautiful and the good is one the interest in which has experienced a powerful revival in the teaching of some of our foremost preachers and writers, the revival may be attributed to many causes. But one cause perhaps stands out more prominently than others. In proportion as the bounds of knowledge are extended, in proportion as new fields are opened up to inquiry and research, and old ones are made to yield new treasures, the essential unity of all human thought becomes more apparent and more striking. It is by means of difference, distinction, dissimilarity among the things which are objects of thought that knowledge makes its first advances. In its later stages its concern is mainly with likeness, similarity, uniformity, the law or order which combines the multitude of parts into a whole. Philosophy, which is the sum of knowledge, inasmuch as it is the expression of the laws of thought, has thus been called a home-sickness. Men run to and fro seeking knowledge, and knowledge is increased. First of all it is a voyage into the manifold, the vast, apparently infinite, variety of things which constitute the universe. Then it is a home-sickness—a movement of return to the one in all, to a recognition of the unity of thought indicative of the unity of mind. So the ideas which predominate in all our modern sciences and investigations are law, order, unity. That partitioning of the mind into various compartments, each, so to speak, supplied with its own machinery and occupied with its own particular industry, that minute partitioning of the mind which was required to suit the condition of human intelligence, when as yet intelligence was concerned chiefly with difference and dissimilarity among things, has been done away in the larger scope of modern thought, much in the same way as the middle wall of partition between Jew and Greek has been done away in Christ. In the make and constitution of the mind there are for us, as there were for the thinkers of ages remote from ours, susceptibilities, impressions and ideas, such as those of the true, the beautiful, the good, which are distinguished from each other. But they are all, as we see, so intimately connected together in the structure of mind itself that to separate them, as they have been separated in earlier systems of thought, seems to us as great a blunder as it would be to ignore the idea of the conservation of force or the law of gravitation. In the study of mind, we find ourselves obliged to recognise so much difference in the quality of our impressions and ideas as to make it possible or necessary to speak of faculties, powers, susceptibilities, distinguishable in a more or less marked manner from each other—that, for example, with which we are concerned in religion from that with which we are concerned in art. These distinctions in the quality of our impressions and ideas being recognised, the unity of thought, the unity of mind, still remains for us a fact, of which every advance of knowledge contributes some further demonstration and illustration. Among the reasons for a revival of interest in the old gospel of the connection of the beautiful and the good this reason is perhaps entitled to prominence. It has thus come to be felt, as it never has been felt before—at any rate not since the days of Plato—that with reference to the cultivation of the beautiful and the good we are concerned with one and the same mind; and further, that, granting some distinction to exist in the mind between classes of impressions and ideas, the beautiful and the good are those which lie nearest to each other and have most in common. Of late it has been much pressed upon the notice of the religious public, especially of people belonging to the straiter sects, that our religion, as far as the beautiful is concerned, is Hebraistic, that the love of beauty paramount among the Greeks, all but inactive even among Hebrews, is little represented in it. The reply of the religious public, or of that part of it belonging to the straiter sects of our religion, is, of course, What does it signify? It is with the good in certain lofty forms that we are concerned in religion; the beautiful is an affair with which we have nothing whatever to do. What is meant, however, by that revival of interest in an old gospel to which I refer is the conviction that in regard to morality and religion we have a good deal to do with the beautiful. How much we have to do with it is therefore a question which it is not by any means a waste of time to discuss.

As to the relation between the beautiful and the good, short work is made of such questions by accepting the definition of the good which is to be found in the Gospel of Christ. To live for others, in the lives of others, a wider, truer, intenser life than that of the selfish mind, is the best of life according to that definition. It is not a commandment given from heaven, with rewards and penalties to give it weight, which makes that the best of life; it is the very nature of things, it is the very make and constitution of human nature. The emotion which is connected with that is life as nothing else is—fulness of life, intensity of life, all that makes life valuable, as emotion of other sorts is not and cannot be. The distinctions between right and wrong, beautiful and vile, noble and ignoble, with which this emotion is concerned, are distinctions to which there are none comparable in importance and weight, and are so, not because of what is written in a book and said to be God's Word, but because human nature is what it is.

Some minds, as we know, are so constituted or so disciplined that while, in regard to matters of taste and beauty, their susceptibility to emotion is extreme, in regard to these distinctions it is dull, or feeble, or dead. Intoxicated easily by the beautiful, or what seems to them beautiful, in some of its forms, they are little affected or not affected at all by what seem the plainest and most forcible dictates of morality and religion, that is to say, by what concerns the good if it be distinguished from the beautiful. But the condition of such minds is not an index to the constitution of mind in general, else instead of having nations convulsed about questions as to the rights of man, we should have their peace disturbed, their trade interrupted, their militias called out, to settle questions as to the superiority of one design for a new church over twenty or a hundred other designs. We should have the ecstasy and sorrow of love, in the experience of most of our race, turning, not upon faithfulness or unfaithfulness, but upon styles of beauty like the Greek, or the Roman, or the Dutch. The idea which the Gospel of Christ gives us as to the best of life is one of which all human observation and experience is the verification—that to live for others, to live in their lives by sympathy, with the quickened emotion of brotherhood, is life at its best and fullest. Life in that form is inclusive, in the widest and truest sense, of the love of love and hate of hate, which is ideal life, spiritual life, eternal life for mortal man. So when we hear that the love of art for art's sake is that which gives the fullest and best experience of life, when we are told in prose and verse that the relation of the beautiful to the good is inverted in all our ordinary ideas of morality and religion, that it is the beautiful first, and not the good, which ought to be our quest in the search for life that shall be life indeed—when we hear this or anything like this we know what to think. What we have to think is not merely that the Gospel of Christ says no. It is that the nature of things, of which the Gospel of Christ is but an expression, says no. If there is to be any distinction at all between the beautiful and the good, one thing is to be considered settled and determined by human experience, and that is, that the good with which we are concerned in morality and religion is that in which the best of life is to be sought and found, no matter what becomes of the beautiful. It is to say the same thing in other words, to say that in the good of religion and morality we are concerned with the beautiful in its highest and best form—that in which there is the fullest experience of life.

Supposing this then to be clear with reference to any gospel of the beautiful as connected with the good, the natural inference would seem to be that there is not very much in this doctrine to concern anybody who is anxious about his own spiritual well-being or that of his fellow-men. If the good is so much better and greater than anything else, why concern ourselves about anything else? There is not time for everything—why not this by itself alone? But very little reflection is required to show that this is exactly what cannot be. Thought, emotion, life is at its best and fullest when it takes the form of living for others as the Gospel of Christ bids us live. That is beyond doubt or question. But as regards human existence in general, this thought, emotion, life, is not the beginning but the end of the story. There is first that which is natural before there is this which is spiritual. It is nearly two thousand years since Christ was preaching His Gospel in Judea. For the greater part of the time since, in every country in which it has been preached it has been misrepresented and misunderstood, if not by the few, certainly by the many. That life for others of which the Gospel is full as a poem is full of imagery, or as a garden is full of flowers, is, in anything like its perfection and beauty, almost as rarely to be seen in a Christian community as in those communities to which we send our missionaries. It might be suspected to be one reason why Christ has been so much preached as altogether other than man, that a difference of nature as great as between God and man seems almost required to account for the difference between His life and that of the multitude calling themselves His disciples. If there is a better appreciation of that life to-day than in Christian countries in mediæval times or times much more recent, it is owing to a general advance of mind, to the increase of civilization, culture, refinement, to the fact that the thoughts of men are advanced with the process of the suns. Mind, the organ of all thought, must be cultivated in order that thought about the good, the beautiful, or the true, may be what it ought to be. You can expect only a partial appreciation of things with which you are concerned in any one department of thought, if the mind with which you have to think is but partially developed; crude morality, crude religion, are inevitable where mental culture in general is poor and restricted. You don't expect the manners or the piety of a gentleman from an ignorant boor or from a Hottentot newly converted to Methodism. There were civilizations before ours. That with which we are made acquainted in what remains of Greek literature and Greek art had many points of excellence as compared with ours, if it had some great blemishes from which ours is free. With regard to that civilization it is easy to see that what it included of the cultivation of the beautiful afforded scope for the cultivation of all the humanities, for a better religion and morality than any that was recognised among the Greeks—scope which we have yet to gain for the development of the Christian religion and Christian morality. If instead of being grafted as it was on the stock of Roman civilization, already in decay, or on the barbarism to which Roman civilization was obliged at last to succumb, the religion of Christ, the morality of the Gospels had been allied with the culture of the Greeks, and both together had made that conquest of the world which was made by the Roman eagles, it is hard to say how different the whole intellectual, moral, religious aspect of the world, at least of the Western world, might have been.

To refer to the idea of evolution, development, which is so much a part of all our modern modes of thought, gives consistency and clearness to this view of things. It is a view of things indeed by which the truth of that idea is strikingly exemplified and illustrated. Religion, according to those modes of thought which are governed by this idea, is itself, in all its forms, the growth of the human soul. There is progress in it from lower to higher forms, the highest conceivable, as we think, being that in which there is the recognition of duty to man as duty to God. This progress of religion, as part of the general progress and development of mind, is dependent upon, and cannot be dissociated from, all that progress to which we give the name of science and art and what not. It is quite true, of course, that, apart from any extraordinary advance in the way of culture, there may be, there has been, the most signal progress in the discovery and revelation of moral and religious truth. That has to be admitted with regard both to Judaism and to Christianity. But it still remains true to the whole experience of mankind that there is an order according to which there is first that which is natural; then that which is spiritual, according to which, therefore, the fate of morality and religion—among human interests the highest—is bound up with that of education and disciplined intelligence. On any view of the origin of our race—except one which history itself proves to be a mistake—it is a long road which humanity has had to travel from the beginnings of thought to that commerce with the skies in the recognition of God as

One and of duty to man as duty to God which is pure and undefiled religion, and in which a perfect morality is implied and contained. It is a long road, and there is much to be done by the way in which it is the poetic or artistic rather than the religious idea of life which is principally concerned. It is not in one line of thought only that the human spirit is so cultivated and enriched that the life of thought becomes, above all, the worship and service of the Eternal. "Whatsoever things are true, whatsoever things are honourable, whatsoever things are just, whatsoever things are pure, whatsoever things are lovely, think on these things"—this is the dictate of pure religion and undefiled. Though your chief quest is religion or morality, though your chief aspiration is after that life which is life indeed in the recognition of duty to man as duty to God, other feelings must be cultivated to give it volume, and must be brought within the scope of it and touched with its intensity.

This, I say, is what accounts for the revival by many of our foremost prophets and teachers with so much earnestness at the present day of that old gospel of which the beautiful is a leading term. It is a gospel, in the first place, which has this to say for itself, in common with another gospel, that the world is one in which glad tidings, especially for the poor, are, or ought to be, sure of welcome. "Consider the lilies of the field how they grow, they toil not, neither do they spin, yet Solomon in all his glory was not arrayed like one of these." Art, which is so much the birth of luxury, is at the best no more than an expression, always an inadequate expression, of the delight of the human soul in the beauty of nature. How much of that delight is it which the conditions of human life, such as they are for millions of the human race, admit of their enjoying when you bid them consider the lilies how they grow? Between the millions of our race whose life is one of poverty and wretchedness, and the contemplation of the beauty of the lilies and all the effects of such contemplation upon the soul, what an interval is placed by the existence of great cities which are what Ruskin has called them—huge ash heaps, with a sky over them which is manufactured below. To give beauty for ashes here would be an undertaking in the way of city improvement which no Town Council has ever yet thought of attempting. Here, where the conditions of human life as regards intelligence, comfort, purity, enjoyment, dignity, everything which makes life valuable, are so unfavourable, so exactly the reverse of what they ought to be, it is hard to say what is to be thought of these conditions, harder still to see what is to be done in the way of altering them. On the moral and religious side, as on the side of social and political order and economy, the questions which arise in regard to improvement or progress are complicated and perplexing, as we see from church congresses, social congresses, sanitary congresses, and from debates in town councils and in Parliament. There are two sides to almost every question, and the questions are many. Vested interests of all sorts, the faults of the poor as compared with other classes, the possible *versus* the impossible as regards anything like a reduction of our social inequalities—all these things are in debate in such a fashion as to leave a vast number of minds in a state of confusion approaching intellectual paralysis. On every side but one on which it is approached the problem is one of almost hopeless obscurity. The most contradictory solutions of it are propounded in the name of morality and religion. It would seem to be only or above all on the side of what concerns the beautiful, not on that of what concerns the good, that the problem is at all soluble, or at any rate that it admits of a clear and definite word being uttered in regard to it. That word is—Be the right or the wrong of all this state of things what it may, in a moral or religious point of view, it is not to be longer endured. It is an offence against God, who made heaven and earth, and made them beautiful, and made man sensitive to the beauty of the earth and of the skies.

Be the fault whose it may, the beauty which there is in nature is conspicuous by its absence in the greater part of human life. In the absence of that beauty, in the presence of all that is ugly, revolting, detestable, human life is hopelessly sick, distempered, distraught in regard to all its issues and all its interests, the highest of all above all. It is the force and clearness of this conviction which is the secret of the earnestness with which a man like John Ruskin preaches the Gospel which was once preached by Plato. It is, or till now it has been, the idea of many people that art and literature of every kind, in which the love of the beautiful is manifested, is for the rich, or at any rate for the idle, for Solomon in all his glory, if by chance the hours hang heavy on his hands, and pastime of some sort is required for him. It is this idea of which we find a lingering trace in ecclesiastical minds much alarmed at the idea of art galleries, museums, and libraries being thrown open on Sunday, now that even the green fields are no longer absolutely forbidden to persons who can walk through a few miles of streets to have a glimpse of them. The idea which John Ruskin and the many cultivated people who read his books, not always with assent to all he says, but always with pleasure and profit, have of the beautiful is exactly the opposite of this. I don't know that he would so express it, but that idea is that art is for the poor, especially for the swarms of human beings who are doomed, instead of passing their lives in the green fields or seeing the lilies, to have only a life-long acquaintance with those huge ash-heaps of ours, the skies of which are manufactured below. Give beauty for ashes, he would say; bring men to the lilies or the lilies to men, if not in nature then in art. What is bare, ugly, revolting in the conditions of human existence, do your best to abolish and to substitute for it what is pleasing and beautiful; that is the only way in which you will have what you want either of peace on earth, and good-will among men, or of glory to God. It is, above all, not with reference to the amusement of the idle few, but with reference to the social, moral, religious refinement and advancement of the toiling and degraded many, that the beautiful has its claims to be considered as among the first and foremost of human interests. This new old gospel of the beautiful which is preached with so much earnestness is something of a gospel of glad tidings for the many. Yet I remark, in conclusion, it is something of the sort, too, for all mankind, for the Jew first, the Jew in point of religious feeling, and afterwards for the Greek, if by that term I may distinguish the rest of mankind from those Christian sects and parties that are characterized by narrowness and exclusiveness in their religious views. There is a well-known and often-quoted passage in the writings of the old Greek philosopher of whom John Ruskin is a devout disciple, the gist of which is given by Professor Jowett in terms brief enough to be given here. An old prophetess is made to speak in this passage, and this is the substance of what she says :—

"I will now initiate you into the greater mysteries, for he who would proceed in due course should first love one fair form and then many, and learn the connection of them, and from beautiful bodies he should proceed to beautiful minds and the beauty of laws and institutions until he perceives that all beauty is of one kindred ; and from institutions he should go on to the sciences, until at last the vision is revealed to him of a single science of universal beauty ; and then he will behold the everlasting Nature which is the cause of all and will be near the end. In the contemplation of that supreme being of love he will be purified of earthly leaven and will behold beauty, not with the bodily eye but with the eye of the mind, and will bring forth true creations of virtue and wisdom and be the friend of God and heir of immortality."

Such were the thoughts of one mind some four hundred years before Christ, thoughts in which the beautiful and the good, nature, art, literature, morality, religion are comprehended in a theory of the beautiful. It is not every mind, perhaps not even every intelligent mind, to which such a theory will not appear to be more of a poetical dream than a consistent account of the interdependence of different departments of thought. But be this as it may, there is truth in it, truth of which most minds can have some glimpses. For the higher education of men and women in the principles and in the practice of morality and religion other emotion than that with which religion is directly concerned requires to be cultivated and brought within the scope of it and raised to its intensity. Our religion, as I have so often said, is spiritual because it is moral ; yet the morality is not given with it except in scattered hints and suggestions. We are thrown back by our religion for our morality, for the conduct of life, upon the source of our religion—upon the soul itself. In the soul itself, as Plato suggests, the beautiful and the good are so much mixed up, their sources lie so near to each other, that it is often rather by asking what is beautiful than by asking what is good that we can settle for ourselves our questions of religion and our questions of morality. Take a simple illustration of what I mean. Lord Chesterfield's politeness or that which is the charm of fashionable society in Paris or in London is not, in the first instance at least, a question of morality, it is a question rather of what is pleasing and beautiful. Not the higher education, or at any rate the highest, is concerned in producing it, but that which is given at so much a term in universities and schools and in the domestic circles in which refinement is indigenous or hereditary. What this product of education is understood in certain circles of society to mean is otherwise expressed by the phrase, "What it is to be a gentleman"; and by that there is understood a great part of any morality of which we can boast either in public or in private life, any of that recognition of duty to man as duty to God, which constitutes religion. It is an illustration of the truth of Plato's conception and Ruskin's conception, that the beautiful and good are more often one than two, that the morality, so to speak, which the moral sense does not supply is furnished to it in distinct form and method from the side of the beautiful. Similar considerations apply to many or most of our social habits, customs, institutions, arrangements. To find out what is good in them, the most direct way is often to ask, how they stand on the score of what is beautiful, how they affect that sense of what is lovely, loveable in and for itself which is so near akin to, so often identical with, righteousness and goodness. Our morality and our religion require improvement. That is beyond doubt. They are in many respects elementary and imperfect. That is so as regards national morality, social morality, all kinds of morality. That the pitch of it should be elevated, that its dictates should be made distinct, recourse must be had to that which lies so near to it in the human soul, the sense of what is beautiful in and for itself.

Hence the poets are the legislators of the future. Would that they were, more than they are, our counsellors and advisers and preachers in the present. With the vision and the faculty divine which they possess above all in regard to the beautiful, they and minds akin to theirs engaged in art and literature, much more than the scientific moralist or theologian, at any rate of the old school, have that help to give us which we most need in striving towards a higher level of being and well-being, including moral and religious being and well-being. It is theirs to show us, after Plato's idea, the scale of beauty rising through fair bodies to laws, institutions, sciences, to the universal and eternal God. It is required for the moralizing of much of our morality and the spiritualizing of much of our religion that much of the love of love and hate of hate which is inspired by the love of the beautiful should be infused into them to give light and guidance to the instincts which are concerned with the good. Teach children the three R.'s, then teach the girls to sew and cook and wash. Hurry the boys, if they are not required to go to work, to a technical school to learn carpentering, tailoring, weaving, engineering, shipbuilding. All that is further required is some instruction in morality and religion :—that is the idea of education, at any rate of education for the million, which is still common, though not quite as common as it has been. No accomplishments, nothing that cannot prove itself to be directly and immediately useful or indispensable ; above all no trifling with poetry or music, or painting, or anything of that sort, in which the love of the beautiful and that merely is concerned. It is an excellent idea of education for a mechanic or a housekeeper. But for a human being, for a man made in the image of God, and not well made unless he have a soul which can be wrapt in the vision of God as the supremely good for him; No! This education if it means anything means just the cultivation of the mind on the side farthest away from, not the side nearest to, virtue and goodness, morality and religion, with the effect that what cultivation of these is directly attempted is poorly rewarded. Consider the lilies how they grow, they toil not, neither do they spin.

It is the beautiful which is nearest akin to the good; cultivate that by all means possible, and as much as you can. If you have it, help to give it to the many who have it not; it is the surest way to bring the good into view and to render the attainment of it practicable. I would settle for my part, if I had the chance, a number of questions which have arisen as to the university training of preachers and teachers of religion in a very simple manner. I would say, the best preachers of religion that I know are not trained theologians. They are poets and men of letters, Plato and Shakespeare, Carlyle and Ruskin among the number. Preachers, as a rule, simply in consequence of their training being that of specialists, have not the art which is just the art they need, to bring emotion of all kinds, above all emotion as to the beautiful, within the scope of the religious emotion, so as to give to it its maximum of volume and its most definite direction. In view of that fact it might be well to prescribe for preachers rather certain extra studies in literature and science, in music, in poetry, painting, than those which are prescribed in theology, in regard to which the Churches cannot agree. For my part I think that would have some practical effect as regards the improvement of preaching, which I suppose is not a little wanted for what is called the deepening of spiritual life. Anyhow, all that I have said amounts to this, that, as regards the gospel of Christ, and the supreme good of that gospel, which is to love God and man, he is not a wise or a prudent man, however he may think himself so, if it has little or no meaning for him to say, "Consider the lilies how they grow"; if his mind is what he would perhaps call practical, exclusive of the influences of art and literature, of thought directed to the beautiful; if he does not give himself the aid in his religious life and in his moral behaviour of the trained and disciplined feeling that, in a sense, the good—the highest good for man—is only another name for what is in itself to the soul supremely beautiful.

VIII.

TO WHOM IT SHALL BE GIVEN.

"Whosoever hath to him shall be given."—Matthew xiii. 12.

WHEN the military chest had to be abandoned in the retreat from Moscow, the French soldiers filled their pockets with its contents—gold coins, as I suppose—but finding as they marched on in the frozen wastes that they could buy nothing with their coins, and being encumbered with the weight, they pitched them away. It is rarely that money in civilized States has so little value as it had for those victims of a crowned madman's frenzy. As a medium of exchange among us, its value is a growing marvel. What strikes the observer of human life is that to him that hath in this one kind there seems to be given of every kind—interest, compound interest, of course—gold lace, pine apples, social position, a cushioned seat in church, a carriage and pair, books, refinement, a happy and contented mind, love, obedience, troops of friends, all that the world and life have to give. After all, however, the world is not so very accommodating and open-handed to the capitalist as it looks, its arrangements are not so exclusively and completely in his favour. Between what a man has in himself and what he has, or may have, outside of himself there is always a distinction of some moment, all-important, indeed, as regards human well-being. That distinction is recognised and respected in the arrangements of this world, according to which it is that to him that hath it shall be given. Relatively to it, that which is thus given may be said to be given strictly in one kind, though it appear to be in ever so many kinds. Get money, and you get with it things as various as pine apples, and a seat in Parliament, or jewellery at a fancy price, and public admiration bestowed literally for nothing. But, in truth, it is only money's worth after all which, in this case, is added to money—the exchange of values is all in one kind. What a man has *in* himself is not necessarily augmented by the augmentation of that which he possesses *outside of* himself, be it all that is included in the biggest American or European fortune. Exactly the opposite may be the effect, as all the satirists of all civilized societies make a point of observing for our edification and amusement; exactly opposite is the effect in the case of that rich man who is so much of a fortune to the second-rate novelist and poet—who, because he is a rich man, looks down as from a place of glory upon the rest of the species—his soul narrowed as his purse is distended. In such a case what a man has in himself, it is obvious to everybody but himself, is contracted in proportion as that which he has outside of him is extended.

Communism is the gospel of stagnation. It is great tidings only for a world near its dissolution—a race with its work all done, and its course just about finished. It is to civilization what the Dead Sea is to Jordan. Whatever else may be said about it, it is an encitement which is needed to direct men and nations into the path of progress, and to keep them in it, that money should make money as it does, that art should produce art, that material advantages should involve and evolve other advantages, that the world should be found to yield interest and compound interest for all sorts of capital. If, as the result of this, evils accrue to men and nations, if property tends to accumulate in a few hands, if the rich become richer and the poor poorer in civilized communities, it is a necessity which has its sad, even its terrible, side. But whatever sadness belongs to it, it is an indispensable condition of the progress of human society. But while it seems best for the world that industry in the acquisition of wealth should be spurred by so large a premium being attached to it, the question for the individual man, under all circumstances, as to making the best of the world and life is never simply how much or how little he is to add to what he has outside of himself. There is another question, which is not one of addition but of subtraction, as Diogenes in his tub compared with Napoleon in all his glory may be quoted to show. The question for the individual may be, not how much he can contrive to add to his resources, but to what point he can reduce the number of his wants. If your wants are as few and simple as those of Diogenes, that which you have may be absolutely little, yet it may be enough for you; if they are unbounded as those of Napoleon, you may have Europe for a kitchen garden. and find it not half big enough. So long as this is the case, it must always be a question for the individual with regard to what is outside of himself, whether his best course is not rather to curtail his wants than increase his possessions. Keep constantly in view a distinction to which this importance at any rate belongs—the distinction between what a man has in himself and what he has outside of himself. You see that it is a real distinction, and the facts of one sphere of human life will be found to illustrate the facts of another, sometimes by comparison and sometimes by contrast. Much more truly and certainly in regard to what a man has in himself than in regard to what he has outside of himself, the law holds good that to him that hath it shall be given. Here the capitalist, large or small, is sure of a return in the shape of interest. There is no such contingency here as there is in those mercantile callings and pursuits in which where there are large profits there are correspondingly heavy losses. Here there is no question of the disproportion between what a man has and what he wants being as well remedied possibly by curtailing his wants as by increasing his possessions. So much scope is there here for desire that no curtailment of it is needed to reduce disproportion. On the contrary, every accession to property here, however desirable in and for itself, is all the more so if it whets the desire for more. Much the largest part of the activity, energy, struggle, and endeavour of the greater number of human beings is misapplied, and therefore wasted, as far as individual happiness and well-being are concerned, just because these considerations as to the difference between what a man has in himself and what he has outside of himself are disregarded, because that is sought in one sphere of things which is not to be had but in another. From this point of view the struggle for existence, which is among us by the struggle for wealth as it grows complicated and intensified to such an extent, more and more eager, hurried, engrossing, becomes to the thoughtful mind in regard to everything but the end to which it is directed, a picture and a parable of what human life ought to be and might be. While competition in every trade is such as to be reckoned among the causes of sudden death and a high rate of mortality, and is thus an indication that, in regard to what is most in request in it, the world is growing narrower for us as it grows older, the thought is all the more strongly brought home to the thoughtful observer of human life and society that a man's life consisteth not in the abundance of things which he possesseth; that the things in which it does consist, if they were competed for, would be found sufficient and superabundant; that as far as these things are concerned, the world grows never narrower but always wider. As far as it is or can be a mental possession for a man—if I may so call it—the world is always the same world for mankind, not larger or smaller in one age than in another, or if ever larger, rather when it is old than when it is young. All the limitations and restrictions to which human life is subject in its relation to material things and to the existing arrangements of human society, vary from age to age; they are greater or less for one class of human beings, or one individual, than for another. What a man has outside of himself is so far beyond his disposal that to increase it as he would like is or may be difficult or impossible. In that respect, in one age and in one place, the individual may find himself, as compared with other individuals, situated more favourably or less favourably. In regard to the world as a mental or spiritual possession it is different. What that shall be to him, much or little, great or small, it is for every individual to determine for himself. To him that hath it shall be given. There are no conditions or limitations but this—you have what you choose to take. All that is or has been, as far as it enters or can enter into the human mind or heart to become a part of its life and being, is always extant, greater rather than less in a later age of the world than in earlier ages. Nothing has been lost, nothing has perished from the world which was ever found in it by those loftier and nobler spirits of our race to whom it has been most glorious and divine. In regard to what concerns the life of the intellect and the life of the soul—that which a man has in himself, and which makes him a conscious being— the world is the same to-day as it has been since man became man, only enriched by age instead of impoverished. Every morning that restores to light what the night concealed, and that recalls the soul of man to consciousness of itself, makes all things new, as new as they were at the dawn of creation, as far as every human soul has an interest in the appropriation of them as an intellectual possession. "Trespassers will be prosecuted"—no such notice has any meaning in *this* universe, or in any part of it, except for vacant minds. The soul is free, as Goethe says, though the foot is clogged. All the facts of nature and of human experience, out of which the thought of the best and greatest of our race created the world as it existed to them, are here in our view, with some perhaps added, which to them were illegible and undecipherable. It is our own fault if our world is not as large or as divine as theirs was, if, indeed, it is not larger and more divine. We are too superstitious, as were the Athenians in the age of Paul and Silas, and our superstition is in regard to men as well as in regard to the gods. Everywhere in the dominion of thought, in the sphere of art and literature, of social and political life, above all of morality or religion, some Caesar or other doth bestride this narrow world as a colossus, and we petty men—the best of us—walk under his huge legs and peep about, I will not say, to find dishonourable graves, but, at any rate, to live lives ignoble because unambitious. We are suspicious of pickpockets, but most of us are scarcely more suspicious of them than of righteous men and prophets who tell us that it is better to see with our own eyes what the world is and what it may be for us, than to live content with as much knowledge of it as the thinking of somebody dead and gone will allow us to have.

If the Parliament of man, of which there is mention in modern verse that is akin to ancient prophesy—if that Parliament had been prematurely convened in the age of Queen Elizabeth, and if the representatives of the intellect and culture of the civilized world had been asked to vote upon the question, whether or not there would ever again be as great a poet as Homer, or Æschylus, or Sophocles, or Euripides, or Virgil, the vote would have been two to one, or many to one against the probability. Yet at that time Shakespeare was at school at Stratford, or meditating the seven ages of man as a play-actor in London. He had but to open his eyes upon that world, the poetic wealth of which was supposed to have been exhausted ages before, to find in it wealth enough—wealth, magnificence, beauty of which no age and no mind had ever dreamed. Now we say there never will be another Shakespeare. It may be true in a sense. Another dramatist like him we may never have—one with such a command of so much picturesque decay— just as we may never have another inventor or improver of the steam engine like James Watt, or a discoverer of gravitation like Sir Isaac Newton.

What is not true, is that we may not have, that we ought not to look for, other Shakespeares to whom as to that incomparable one the world in its poetical wealth shall be inexhausted and inexhaustible. It would be absurd of course to compare Wordsworth and Shakespeare as poets. A brilliant literary critic, such as I could name, could give us a score of reasons for not naming these two names together. But in point of fact the unexpected is that which happens in Wordsworth, just about as much as in Shakespeare, in regard to the discovery of new sources of poetical emotion. Admirers of Wordsworth say there will never be another Wordsworth, and so it may be. Only just as we have actually had Shakespeare, and then Wordsworth, the chances are, nay, the certainty is, that we shall have, not perhaps Shakespeare after Wordsworth, or even Wordsworth after Wordsworth, but creation after creation, out of the old material of a new heaven and a new earth for the poetic mind. Here is no question merely of what is called creative genius—a misleading term, since, in point of fact, if there is any art to the practice of which genius is not addicted, it is creation. In literature and art the failures are creations. The same world of tears and smiles, of ecstatic joy, and speechless woe, of victories, and of foiled ambitions, of heroic purpose and maiden grace and tenderness, the same world in which the soul of Shakespeare expatiated as a bird in air, exists for you and me. So does the world in which Wordsworth meditated morning, noon, and night, and of which his meditations were sweet and sublime. It is an enchanted isle; have Prospero's mind and you can restore it all.

That which Shakespeare and Wordsworth had of the seeing eye and the understanding heart is shared by you and me if we can read their writings with any appreciation. Have so much of that, of what they had, and in that measure there is given to you what was given to them. To him that hath it shall be given. Only bring to nature and life something of mind as free as mind should be, and you shall find them not sparing of their gift. Not only in regard to literature, art, science, the end of which is thought, but in regard to thought and feeling, in which the practical interests of men and nations are involved, to have in oneself something which is real at all, or worth anything, is to be in the way of having much. To have a position of influence in a country like this, such as the youngest burgess* of the city occupies, is much for a man to have. It is a larger share of what the world and life have to give, than the position

* John Bright, on whom the "Freedom of the City" had recently been conferred.

of a Lancashire millowner whose whole property is his mill. Without prejudging the question between those who admire him most and those who admire him least or not at all, I may say, I think that that position only represents in a kind of half-intelligible cypher what really has come to that man as the result of his having had in himself something more and higher than a wish for the acquisition of wealth. Forty or fifty years ago if any man was going to be a patriot—here in England—if any man thought of following in the footsteps of Pym and Hampden, it might well have seemed that he could not possibly make a worse start than as an apostle of peace, calling nations to repentance and the confession of their sin in regard to the corn laws. The office of patriot being vacant, as it always is—at any rate it is never completely filled up—notice, it might have seemed to most men, might have been given in these terms, "No Quaker or adherent of the Manchester School need apply." But the man whom we have just seen among us, laden with honours in his old age, had something in him beyond and above what was mercenary and selfish. See what has been given him. I don't mean in the shape of honours, but of that satisfaction, that interest in living, that intellectual and moral wealth which men who live for their country and for mankind must have whenever—and that is seldom if ever—they have not lived in vain. To him that hath it shall be given, even where all the materials with which a man is armed seem to have been used up, even in a career of which he has received notice that it is no longer open.

In speaking of John Bright I have not been trenching upon politics. But I turn from him to religion, as to that subject which is best worth talking about, not here on Sunday more than in any other place or at any other time. It is here above all that to him that hath it shall be given. It is here, too, above all, that it chiefly concerns us whether it is so or not.

More or less in every sphere of thought and activity, the inducement which a man has to cultivate what nature has given him in the shape of power and faculty, is that the reward is great. Much is given to him that has. That inducement is strong here as it is nowhere else. Augustine, it is said, when he failed as a lawyer, took the infinite for his career. As far as the infinite is synonymous with religion it is a term for a career which is open to every man, and in which success is no question of chance but one of effort and endeavour. In regard to religion, as in regard to every other department of human life, there is, of course, a difference between man and man, between class and class, people and people, generation and generation. By nature one man has much of what you call religious feeling, another man little. That is a fact not to be ignored. But whatever a man has in this kind, be it little or much, there is this inducement to cultivate it, that as far as, by putting it into exercise and so really possessing himself of it, he can be said to *have* it, much is given to him in it and with it, much in proportion to what he already has. Every step forward and upward in that career of Augustine's—the infinite—the wider and greater is the prospect which for the soul is not prospect but property. How does this apply —if at all—to the time in which we live rather than to some ancient time or all ancient time together? I answer that question this morning by referring to the time of which we read here in this Gospel, the time of Christ—the time when he had to tell his disciples, as in this particular passage of Matthew, that it was given to them and not to the multitude to understand the mysteries of the kingdom of heaven. "I speak to them in parables," the Master says, "because they"—that is the multitude, or, as we would say, the general public— "because they seeing see not; and hearing they hear not, neither do they understand. And in them is fulfilled the prophecy of Isaiah, which saith, By hearing ye shall hear, and shall not understand,

and seeing ye shall see, and shall not perceive: for this people's heart is waxed gross, and their ears are dull of hearing, and their eyes they have closed; lest at any time they should see with their eyes and hear with their ears, and should understand with their hearts, and should be converted, and I should heal them. But blessed are your eyes, for they see: and your ears, for they hear. For verily I say unto you, That many prophets and righteous men have desired to see those things which ye see, and have not seen them; and to hear those things which ye hear, and have not heard them." That is the Master's commentary upon his own statement that to him that hath shall be given—the commentary immediately following the text. It is his sermon upon that text, I might leave it to speak for itself in regard to the times in which we live and the generation of which we are a part. He that hath ears to hear let him hear. These things are an allegory of which the meaning, one would say, is difficult to miss. Isaiah's times are a parable for Christ's, and Christ's are a parable for ours. He that runs may now read the application of the parable, because in our time more than in any other the idea is familiar to most minds, that whatever the world in its spiritual aspects has been to any human soul, even the loftiest, it is still. This idea is familiar to our minds in the shape of the truth, or rather truism, that all religion whatever is the outcome of the soul of man communing with the soul of all that is. As there are in history, which is the history of civilized mankind, ages of torpor and inactivity in regard to art and literature, so there are such ages in regard to religion. Account for them how you will, there they are. So too there are ages of movement, change, excitement revolution. Isaiah's was one of these. Christ's was another. Ours—it will be admitted—is a third. In ages like these what may be seen in some fashion at all times, as to the operation of the law that to him that hath it is given, is conspicuously visible. It was so in Christ's time. Those who had eyes saw wonders, those who had ears were astonished at what they heard. In other words the new religious doctrine of the Master, which yet was not new but old, was for as many as were prepared to receive it, for as many as were gifted with exceptional sincerity and earnestness, the revelation of a new heaven and a new earth. To him that hath it shall be given has here its first historical application. Its latest is what concerns us most. It would be idle, and perhaps to some minds impertinent, to compare our own times too closely with those times in this respect. But a comparison, so far, is, I think, possible, which is instructive without being offensive. Now, as then and always, the question with regard to religion is with some minds —I will not say the best, but certainly the openest to conviction—the question is with them of righteousness, the question of the book of Job, Is God just, is the eternal order of the world chance, or a fate which is not blind, a Nemesis which never halts; is that order moral, is it just? With other minds the question, the great question in regard to religion, is of privilege, of happiness here and hereafter. I speak of course in the most general terms in saying so. But there is such a distinction among minds for which religion is any question at all. Keep it in view and it will explain much as to people seeing or not seeing with their eyes, hearing or not hearing with their ears, when new views, or what are called new views of religion, are in question either in times of which we read in history or in the times in which we live. In our time, as in Christ's time, and in the time of Isaiah, it is easy to see that as the result of the old religious questions being asked over again as to the world and God and man's life and destiny —asked over again as they must be in new circumstances—the question with regard to religion is emphasized for us as a question of righteousness, of faith working by love. It is not what you believe about the Trinity, but what is your feeling as to right and wrong, truth and falsehood, humanity and inhumanity. Old religious beliefs, acceptable to the multitude in all ages because, however unthinkable and unbelievable, they offered salvation and happiness, have become questionable to us as to no other age, not only on intellectual but even more on moral grounds. Our estimate of righteousness will not allow us to retain these beliefs unmodified. Whether it be the whole of religion or not, and certainly it is a great part of it, if you have something of this regard for righteousness which enters so largely into religious movements in our time what follows? In the first place, it sets aside for you, we shall say, those old religious beliefs of which I have spoken. But in doing so it does no harm—it does good. Consider how old religious beliefs are set aside for us, if they are set aside at all. It is on the ground that all that is of that kind has had one and the same origin—the soul of man. I say, therefore, with regard to all these old beliefs—the devil and hell for example—however incredible and unthinkable to me, what are they but representations and expressions of the thought, and feeling, and experience of mankind, of millions of human beings like myself? Whatever truth there is in them, if any (and there is sure to be some), is enforced to my mind by the fact that there is so much experience to attest it. All that they mean is that it is the misery of miseries, not to be unfortunate, but to be unjust, impure, unloving. To minds that are alive, as I say, to the question of righteousness as the great question of religion, old religious beliefs —not one set of them, but the whole of them— may be thus absurd and yet true, in form incredible, perhaps revolting, in substance so valid and real that heaven and earth shall pass away before them. And, again, if you have what of the spirit of righteousness, of humanity, the time would seem fitted to endow you with as the spirit of religion, how large a world it opens up for you in that life of mankind in which it is yours to live. These old religious beliefs that are now in decay did but for the most part divide mankind here into the sheep and the goats; they anticipated the day of judgment as a day of wrath, and held out no prospect of a life worth living to the lover of righteousness except in a distant, and it must be said in a circumscribed, heaven. Love righteousness, hate iniquity, as Christ did, as Isaiah did, as your own age, in the spirit of it, expressed by its best minds bids you do, then not in a distant heaven but in this old England and in this old world, with all the good and the evil in it, you will find as much as heart can desire to engross your mind and to stir and fill your life with interests, hopes, fears, aspirations, endeavours in which there is life indeed. To him that hath it shall be given. That same world of divine joy and divine sorrow, in which Christ lived, in which Isaiah lived before him, in which all have lived that have lived not in vain—that same world exists for us. Nothing has faded out of it. Nothing can pass away from it. To him that hath in him but a little of what is kindred to the best of it, much of it shall be given.

IX.

PRESENT OPPORTUNITIES.

"Now is the accepted time, now is the day of salvation."—
2 Cor. vi. 2.

APART altogether from ideas of God and of a future life of which use has been made to promote religion by terror, the present time, in a religious point of view, is mistaken when it is despised, and its opportunities overlooked and neglected.

The drawing of even the poorest artist, with its cottages or castles built upon air, with trees which lean towards us or away from us at impossible angles, the branches of which resemble no branches that ever grew, may be accepted as a certain witness to reality, a kind of testimony to the existence of such things as houses and trees. If these things had not really existed, they would never have been drawn so badly. What professes to be a musical performance is to your ears perhaps only a prolonged intolerable discord. But even that discord may be quoted as showing that there is such a thing as harmony, of which it is only a blundering representation. Were there no such thing as "linked music long drawn out" there would be no attempts of tuneless singers and unskilled performers to make life pleasant. In the same way, perhaps, we may without much trouble find a certain testimony to truth, a certain reflection of reality in the wildest harangues of newly converted preachers of the gospel warning us to flee from the wrath to come, and in regard to that wrath declaring that the present instant is the only opportunity of salvation. There is a certain truth in these attempts to further godliness by terror—they bear a kind of witness to the fact that in respect of what is spiritual, life is an opportunity which may be used or wasted, but which at any rate cannot return, of which the past is past and can never be recalled, with regard to which it is impossible to conceive that in any other state of being than this, to human consciousness anywhere or anyhow continued, the message to the soul can ever, in any sense, be repeated, "*Now* is the accepted time, now is the day of salvation." Considered not with reference to eternal rewards and punishments in another state of being, but with reference to the spiritual, the eternal order of the world, this present life, not in spite of its being not all spiritual, but just because it is not, is rich in spiritual opportunities and advantages of which it is impossible to conceive the repetition. It is not possible, as I daresay most of us believe, to speak of the destiny of mankind as irrevocably fixed in every case in regard to eternal blessedness and misery by what happens here in the few brief and bewildered years of this mortal life. I do not believe it possible to speak of this without going dangerously near to blasphemy. But if we conceive of human existence as continued beyond the present world only in a spiritual form, apart—that is to say, from those bodily, material conditions which exert so powerful an influence upon it here and now—then with reference to that purely spiritual world, the spiritual opportunities of this present life, as far as it is not purely spiritual, can never be recalled.

When Europe, in spite of most of its nations professing the Christian faith, was characterized by the reign of violence, when robbery and murder were trades of which honest men were not ashamed, when barons were captains of bandits and their castles were fortresses and dens of thieves —there rose suddenly, out of the defencelessness of women and the outrages to which they were liable, the institutions of chivalry. By these institutions gallantry and piety were associated, knights in armour went forth to redress the wrongs of women wherever they could be heard of, the most stately and elaborate forms of courtesy and deference to women were exacted at the sword's point from ages addicted to cattle-lifting and familiar with the harrying of villages and towns. In respect to the progress of civilization and of religion, the relation of the weaker to the stronger sex, which dictated in lawless ages the songs of wandering minstrels, and the deeds of doughty knights, retains its influence. It is the chief factor in the progress of both the one and the other. At any rate, in a rough way, you may perhaps more fairly estimate your civilization and your religion in a country like this by reference to the social position of women than by any other test or standard—by considering on the one hand how many convictions there are or ought to be at the police-courts for wife beating, and on the other hand how enviable is the place which women hold in most homes pretending to refinement or Christianity.

If religion, salvation, whatever you choose to call it, is more a matter of a heart right with God than of anything else—that is to say, of the recognition of duty to man as duty to God—if this is a part, a great part of that conformity to the spiritual order of the world, which is salvation and eternal life, the relation of man to woman and of woman to man has much to do with it, and can make or mar human life in regard to it to a larger extent than almost anything else. If in relation to his mother or sister or sweetheart or wife, a man who according to his religion ought to be humane, capable of pity, magnanimous, gentle, forgiving, remains a churl, a petty despot, selfish, mean, exacting, ungenerous, there is little or no hope of that man's salvation.

Abstract arguments in favour of religion—the kingdom of God, an ideal humanity—ought, perhaps, to have overwhelming weight with us, with all mankind. But in point of fact they have not. Our best teachers of the highest religious truth are the influences kindred to air and sunshine that meet us in our homes, that look out upon us from the eyes we love, that smile upon us from the lips of those who are dearer than life. It is easy, therefore, to throw away life and salvation along with life, the next world, if it be purely spiritual, along with this world, not by dissenting from a system of doctrine of which we do not understand the terms, or going irregularly to church where there is the opportunity of doing penance after the Protestant manner by patiently enduring a tedious discourse, but by an ungoverned temper, by allowing selfishness to prevail against generosity and kindness in the relations of home, and friendship, and love. Considering how difficult it is to practise the humanity, the patience, the meekness which it is easy to preach as salvation and eternal life, blessed is the man who knows how to take advantage of the opportunity of practising it where it is least difficult, in the sphere of those relations which subsist between the stronger and the weaker sex, blessed is the man who daily in that sphere learning to be gentle, honourable, patient, kind, compassionate, is disciplining himself for the society of the just made perfect in love and pity. If a man throw away all this opportunity by making his home a place where an unkind, capricious tyrant displays his power to make those dependent on him unhappy, he could not perhaps otherwise more completely make shipwreck of the faith and throw away his chance of salvation. At any rate it is not conceivable that any purely spiritual state of being can ever give him a better chance of salvation than that which he has thus enjoyed and discarded.

What is true of one relation in which human beings are placed to each other in this life, is true of many or of most relations: those of them that are least spiritual in their nature are not those which afford the smallest opportunities, but the largest, of spiritual cultivation—that is, properly understood, of salvation.

It may not, of course, in any given particular instance happen to be the case, but, as a rule, when one reads and hears of large sums of money being left by a last will and testament for a charitable or religious purpose—for the founding, perhaps, of an institution to be called by the testator's name, and to perpetuate longer than brass the testator's inglorious memory—when one reads or hears of large sums of money left in this way, it is impossible not to feel that some of those who have bequeathed them may have been all their lives, or a great part of their lives, occupied in throwing away their own best chance of salvation. It cannot be said, of course, without reserve or qualification, that large sums of money, hundreds of thousands of pounds, ought never to be found in one man's hands, or that a man may not sometimes properly accumulate his money all his life in order to devote the whole of it to a favourite purpose when he is in the article of death. But it is to be doubted whether these great sums left for charitable and religious purposes do not often represent the foolish parsimony of men who threw away life to gain a monument, who were dead even when they lived, whose hearts were insensible to the claims of humanity, who had never learned to put out their wealth, as regards what is better than wealth, to any kind of usury. As far as this may be supposed to be the case, these big sums, perhaps bequeathed to promote the salvation of future ages, represent the fact that the testators threw their own salvation away. It is not in the sphere of what is ecclesiastical or purely spiritual that rich men, any more than poor men, can make their spiritual calling and election sure, it is in the sphere of trade and commerce and the intercourse of daily life. It is perhaps more in seeming than in fact that, when a rich man hears what professes to be religious truth, the gospel, the word of life, and pays no attention to it, acts as if he never heard it, falls asleep in the act of listening to it, he misses his chance of salvation. But what is perfectly certain with regard to a rich man is, that appeals are made to his sympathies by certain of the great evils of this life for which money is the cure, or of which it furnishes the means of alleviation. In an evil world, one of the evils of which is poverty, in a world not altogether spiritual, where rags are uncomfortable, and children scream if they are hungry, and starved mothers clasp starved infants to their breasts, a constant demand upon his sympathies is made in the case of the rich man just because he is rich; and if it be salvation, as it certainly is represented in the gospel to be, to have a human heart, to pity and bless and save, it is above all in the way in which he responds to this appeal and allows his natural sympathies to go out to meet it, that the rich man forgets or remembers his day of salvation. What is true of the rich man's opportunities of salvation is true of the poor man's; the best of them in a spiritual sense are often not ecclesiastical or religious but social. It is not a matter, I think, of astonishment, however much it may be of regret, that religion in every form which it takes among sects at different periods of time, should not be attended with the results anticipated from it among the industrial and the poorer classes of a community like this. If a working man or a struggling merchant is led to believe that his spiritual destiny was fixed in eternity, or that it depends upon a miracle of some sort, to which no calculation can be applied, it can scarcely surprise us should he be found occupying his mind, in the meantime, with the cares of this world, which will not suffer themselves to be neglected, rather than with anxieties which may possibly be fruitless in regard to another. Even at the best, make religion as spiritual as you please, it has much to contend against in the mind of a man to whom this life is a struggle to live. Apart from the conditions and circumstances and events of actual life among the poor calling for that love to God and man which is salvation, no wonder if your voice is that of one crying in the wilderness, or, rather, at the corners of the streets where hundreds of voices drown each other. But in the lives of the poor, in their relations with each other and with those who show them sympathy, in their experience of want and sickness and neglect, and in the response which suffering makes to suffering, deep answering to deep in human life—in all this, human nature on its better and nobler side, that of patience and goodness and love, has that chance of cultivating itself which is the chance of salvation. Many an individual belonging to those great masses of working men in a community like this who are unknown in the inside of Christian churches— many a man belonging to these lapsed masses who sulkily hears, and perhaps sulkily believes, that to sit by his fireside on a Sunday instead of going twice to church is to throw away his chance of salvation, would be better advised if he were told and if he believed that his best chance of salvation is what he neglects and rejects in choosing to be a surly husband, a bad neighbour, a bad servant or shopmate, a faithless friend, in caring for nobody and being content that nobody should care for him.

Through the whole web of our relations in this life the thread of that which is most spiritual is woven into that which seems of a nature least akin to it. The sacred books of our religion, as of other religions, are filled with exhortations and commandments in regard to common-place duties and obligations. Husbands, love your wives; servants, obey your masters; children, honour your parents; let the young reverence the old—all these exhortations, injunctions, are indications and expressions of the fact that that which is not spiritual in our life is full of spiritual opportunity.

Now is the accepted time, and now is the day of salvation. Not as we might wish it to be, but exactly as it is, life is rich in opportunities of a spiritual kind which are opportunities of salvation. It is not on sacred occasions or in connection with ecclesiastical institutions, or within the sphere of that which is purely spiritual, but in our everyday lives, in the ordinary common-place relations of earthly common-place existence, that there is given to us, above all, and that there is accepted or refused by us, the chance of that spiritual improvement which is salvation. Imagine a state of being in another world in which human existence will be purely spiritual, all earthly physical conditions and properties being extruded from it; whatever it may be and whatever it may include, that state of being will not give any of us those opportunities and advantages which this present despised and calumniated life gives, which the infirmities and sorrows and sins belonging to it afford us, of being what we ought to be, of knowing what we ought to know, of enjoying what we ought to enjoy, as regards what is spiritual. The future of this life will not give us exactly what the present is offering. To-morrow will not bring back what to-day brings. Now is the accepted time, and now is the day of salvation.

That is true of life at all times, under all conditions. That, I remark in a single word in conclusion, is especially true of it in some respects worth notice in our own day, viz., as regards the spiritual opportunities which are hidden in ordinary things and in common-place relations. On the one hand the increase of knowledge, the progress of civilization, has been favourable to the growth of spiritual religion, of Christianity, not in forms to which ages of superstition debased it, but in the form in which it first of all proved itself divine by divine power over the human soul—of Christianity, the first and last word of which is not sacrifice but mercy. Thou shalt love the Lord thy God with all thy heart, and with all thy soul, and thy neighbour as thyself. Never perhaps was there a period in the history of the world in which it was so clearly, so widely, so intelligently understood and upon grounds of reason, rather than authority, that what is required of us by religion is not to be something other than human, but to be what our better nature orders us to be—is not right belief or right worship but right life, above all, is that humanity of which the chief part is to be human. In this respect the order of the world has been the same for all generations. But we have the advantage such as no other age, possibly not even any Christian age, has enjoyed, of seeing what that order is—of breathing as it were in the common air the spiritual inspiration regarding it, which in other days reached only favoured souls at favoured hours. We belong to a time which, religiously as well as otherwise, has its own difficulties and distractions, but undoubtedly the common-place, respectable Christian, the ordinary church-goer now sees more clearly and knows more certainly than his predecessor in other ages that he is under no kind of arbitrary government in this world, that it is sure that whatsoever a man sows he also reaps—that life is not a lottery but an education; that he has no heaven to hope for, and no hell to fear except that which is connected with being true or false to the better nature within him. In this respect, for one thing, now is the accepted time, and now is the day of salvation. There is an advantage as regards salvation in knowing what it is and where to look for it, and we have that advantage along with our fathers, but to a greater extent than they.

Still further, let me merely hint in a word or two, that along with that knowledge of salvation as identical with the truer, nobler humanity of the Christian religion which has now reached the common mind, much else has come which is favourable to the development of that humanity that is favourable to salvation. It is still possible for Christian nations to offer thanksgivings for the horrors of war, and for Christian sects to call the eternal Lord of heaven and earth to witness that they are faithful to ancient hatreds and animosities. Even in our own country there is still much in the relation of class to class which is shown to be wrong by the suspicion and jealousy and bitterness of which it is the chronic occasion. But thanks to the progress of knowledge, to the intercourse of nation with nation in the arts of peace, to many causes besides religion, and to religion itself, there is now undoubtedly a clear and intelligent recognition on the part of the mass of mankind in a Christian country like this, of the brotherhood of man, of the unity of society, of the community of interests which ought to bind together classes and nations in the bond of mutual good-will; there is a recognition of this such as we should look for in vain in history ever since the days when the disciples at Jerusalem had all things in common, and Ananias and Sapphira suffered the penalty of death for lying to the Holy Ghost about private property. The time is favourable as never time in this world was to your finding expression for your religious sentiments, to your looking for your salvation, in that devotion of yourself not to selfish aims but to the good of others which is following Christ, and in which is indeed salvation. If you had lived in other ages, you might have been diverted by the spirit of them from salvation, as far as that means Christ-like humanity, to something very like condemnation, as far as that means intolerance and iniquity. The spirit of this age is in favour of your making your religion as well as all your thoughts and activity an offering to God in the form of effort to promote the wellbeing of man. It recognises in mankind, as claiming your sympathy and deserving your pity, much which the spirit of other ages judged more harshly, to which it played not the good Samaritan but the Pharisee and the Levite. Better than any other time, your time understands it to be true that pure worship is to visit the fatherless and the widows in their affliction, to have a heart to which nothing human is alien, to which the suffering of others is a burden of sorrow, and the gladness of others is a song of spring. A time like this, which turns the thought of the commonplace householder and seatholder upon the weaknesses and sorrows and sins of his kind here, which makes or tends to make a good Samaritan out of every ratepayer, is an accepted time. Whatever a state of being in another world may be to which these weaknesses and sorrows and sins are unknown, it will never give us an opportunity such as the present gives us of learning those universal Christ-like sympathies for which salvation is another name. Now is the accepted time, now is the day of salvation.

X.

A MULTITUDE OF THE HEAVENLY HOST.

" And suddenly there was with the angel a multitude of the heavenly host praising God, and saying, Glory to God in the highest, and on earth peace, good will toward men."—Luke ii. 13, 14.

"THEY all shall wax old as doth a garment, and as a vesture thou shalt fold them up and they shall be changed," is always true of the heavens and of the earth, true to human thought, in which and for which they exist. The sum of knowledge with regard to them is that it is only to mind that they exist. What co-existence, what unity they have, is in the unity of the thinking principle which is concerned in noting at once what is changeful in them and what is constant. Gravitation is not so much the force which binds them together and makes a system or universe of them, as thought, of which gravitation is a product. It is true, therefore, that they all do wax old as a garment, and as a vesture are folded up and changed—for the mind changes in which and for which they exist. Human thought, because it is not independent of human life, continueth not in one stay. Following the vicissitudes of human experience, and determined by the progress of the human mind, modes of thought and of expression change from age to age in the life of nations, change also in the same way, though not perhaps to the same extent, in the life of individuals. So it is to all of mortal kind with hearts to feel, as to the distracted king, that the heavens themselves are old. The heavens and the earth of our fathers, and their fathers, are old for us, for us as a vesture is folded up or changed they are changed and folded up. The old modes of thought and expression are displaced by the action of the unresting mind for which all that is exists, and it is as if there had appeared a new heaven and a new earth in the new modes of thought and expression which it finds for itself.

Life is renewed, according to the Hindu idea of the transmigration of souls, in an unending circuit—the quantity of it never diminished or increased, the form only altered. According to the quality and tenor of the life which has been lived by it in the human form, the soul after the death of the body, and before returning to the human form, is fated to inhabit the body of this or that creature lower or higher. This is the Hindu idea of transmigration—life flowing in an unending circuit, the atoms of which change their places, the volume of which is neither diminished nor increased. There is a certain dim reflection of the truth of things in this idea which, like the painted glass of a cathedral window, is the more impressive for being dim. It is an anticipation of the doctrine of the conservation of force, of which so much is heard in modern science, applied not to matter but to mind. One and the same mind it is which comes into being, in every generation of men, but it is always under changed conditions, and the effect is, must be, to change the heavens and the earth, more or less to antiquate modes of thought and modes of expression with regard to them. In the Hindu doctrine of transmigration the stealer of grain has his punishment in becoming a rat—with, one must infer, his view of the heavens and of the earth curtailed to suit his altered condition. In successive ages in the life of nations, at different stages in the life of individuals, if not to this extent, or in this fashion, yet in a fashion and to an extent of which the doctrine of transmigration is a dim pictorial representation, the heavens and the earth are to the mind what the mind makes them.

Some 1500 years after the birth of Christ, in a

sort of surreptitious manner, the true theory of the motion of the heavenly bodies was announced to the world by Copernicus. Galileo, Kepler, Newton, came in succession to fulfil the movement of thought in which the discovery of Copernicus made so great an epoch. Corresponding to that movement there has come that in which on this solid globe of earth all is seen to be a process of evolution. So the heavens and the earth have been changed to our thought as if they had been made new. Our modes of thought and of expression are our own, and where they differ from those of former ages the explanation is to be sought in history. Thus the idea with which we are now so familiar, though it would have seemed strange to other ages—the idea that all religion has one source, the spirit of man in quest of spirit in the universe answering to itself—this idea, instead of emptying of their meaning all modes of thought and expression, helps wonderfully to restore to them the meaning which they have in course of time lost. I know that this is the very opposite of what is thought by many people. But the reasons which can be given in favour of its truth are too many and too cogent to be set aside. This is the Sunday before Christmas, and we are reminded by that fact how much the thoughts of the Christian world to-day and for some days to come will be turned to the birth of Christ. Modes of thought and of expression in reference to that ineffable event, of which there is a record in these Scriptures dating from comparatively near the time, are current still. In one sense they are as current as ever. For the Church catholic and universal, the heavens and the earth wax not old, nor as a vesture are they folded up or changed. The old narrative is repeated without variation, of how the birth at Bethlehem was heralded from heaven, and how it was marked and noted upon earth. The old modes of thought and of expression in regard to nature and the supernatural, or connected with it, are as current now as they were ten or fifteen or eighteen centuries ago. Yet, what is certain, is that much must since have happened affecting their significance. The human mind has changed, and with it the fashion of the heavens and of the earth. By reason of the truth which is in them, modes of thought and expression may keep possession of the mind for ages, yet not that possession in a later age which they had at an earlier. We still speak the language of the Ptolemaic system of astronomy, though we have accepted the Copernican, when we say that the sun rises and sets. In the process of adjusting itself with the truth of things as it is now conceived by the mind, the truth there was and is in old modes of thought and expression is insensibly refashioned. That there was and is truth in them is what is to be presumed, only in having had to adjust itself to other truth and to take its place in the unity of thought for which the heavens and the earth exist, it may have so been modified and changed as to be found only when search is made for it, not in the letter which killeth but in the spirit which maketh alive. Much must have happened, I say, much has happened since our customary modes of thought and expression about the most wonderful event in history were finally fashioned and determined—much has happened, I mean, affecting, necessarily affecting, their significance to the mind that now is and for which the heavens and the earth now exist. It is always true to human thought that millions of spiritual creatures walk the earth unseen both when we sleep and when we wake. " He maketh the winds his angels and the flaming fire his servant." In human history and human experience it is always as if the unseen must at times become visible to satisfy the demands of the human spirit for converse with its kith and kin beyond the veil of nature—to answer to the needs of man's world of thought and feeling with all that belongs to it of pity and of terror. As much in other speech as in that of the people whose literature we now call the Bible, the angels come and go between heaven and earth. But in that distant age to which the Christian world looks back at this time of the year with so much yearning and sacred gladness — at that time, as by no means since, the ministry of angels was familiar to the human mind — was required to answer, in fact, the necessities of human thought. On occasions infinitely less important than the birth of one whose name should be called Jesus, the Saviour, the angels then came and went in the universe freely because in mind and for mind the universe was what it was. Since then not one has come. So the impression which was made by its being said that this event, among other wonders attending it, was made illustrious by the attendance of a multitude of the heavenly host, and by their jubilation being audible to the ears of shepherds on the plains of Bethlehem — the impression which was made then by that being said, and that which is made now, cannot be altogether the same. With all our ideas of the universe to adjust to it, it is infinitely more wonderful now than it was then. As it is so much more wonderful, it is so much more difficult to realize in thought, to have what truth there is in it present to the mind as actual in regard to the universe in which we live and move and have our being. And so it is with reference to all else that is wonderful in the story of that birth to which the thoughts of the best part of the human race go back as to no other event in all human history. The modes of thought and of expression with regard to all that are unchanged by the lapse of ages—in the letter unchanged—but are they actually the same in spirit to us as they were in another age under cruder and almost opposite conditions of human thought?

I shall endeavour to answer this question as fairly as may be, remembering that all minds are not alike prepared for such discussions, not forgetting, either, that it is only at the best in the most partial and unsatisfactory fashion that such questions can be discussed in the compass of a sermon. The spirit of the age, then, let me say, is what it is—not hostile to religion but certainly antagonistic to the supernatural, or, at the most, dully receptive of it. It is what it is very much on account of the progress of critical and historical studies, some results of which are known to almost everybody, while anything like an exact acquaintance with them is still confined to the few; this progress, again, being more or less dependent upon or connected with the revolution effected in our modes of thought by the progress of physical science. Suppose, then, that as one result of these studies, some such ideas as these are familiar to the majority of educated and thoughtful minds—that the gospels were first written long after the apostolic age, that they represent events in the form best adapted to the exigencies of an age in which the Christian Church, divided against itself by Jewish and Gentile feeling, had to struggle for existence against heathenism, to which all existing culture as well as all political power and supremacy belonged, and that in this an explanation is to be found of the shape which one gospel after another assumed, and of the order in which late in the second century they were finally arranged as we have them. Suppose these ideas, as to the origin and composition of the gospels to be common or widely diffused and entertained, so that it should be seen to be a matter of great significance that in one gospel—that according to Mark—which with good reason on other grounds may be supposed to have been the first of the series to see the light, there should be no account at all of the event which is commemorated at Christmas. Suppose that it is made thinkable or feasible to many minds that the reason why, with so much circumstance, we have in the first and third gospels what we have not in the second, an account of the birth of Jesus, may be that, in the struggle for existence of the Christian Church, the difficulty was more felt at a later than at an earlier time, of advancing the religion of Christ as that of one crucified as a malefactor, and that in proportion as this difficulty was more felt at one time than another, the thoughts and feelings of Christian believers were turned to whatever tradition, or sentiments, or arguments, or inferences from existing scriptures or prophecies seemed to afford ground for an exhibition of the Saviour of the world as a divine being. The religions to which the Christian religion was opposed in the whole heathen world claimed divine origin, named among their founders divine beings. All in Christian sentiment and tradition that assigned that rank to the Saviour of all mankind had thus its time for asserting itself as the truth of the Christian religion. Suppose these ideas familiar to many minds, and, indeed, to all intelligent minds, the significance to these minds must be great of the suggestion that it was owing to its not containing an account of the birth of Jesus that Mark was placed second among the gospels, and that, instead, one was placed first in which the story of it appears, so that ever since the gospels were arranged as they are now there is to be read a continuous history of which the miraculous is the starting point. Here is a mode of thought, then, critical, not to say sceptical, which is very different from that which was common, not to say two thousand years ago, but even twenty years ago, Shall we make any account of it, or ignore it as something of which the least said is soonest mended? I shall not argue the point, I shall merely say that it is better to face it than to shut our eyes to its existence. There is this fact, then, to which the existence of this mode of thought in our time calls attention. If its results are to show that, as regards ancient modes of thought and expression, some difference and distinction must be made and allowed for between the letter and the spirit, between the idea and the fact, between exact history and more or less variable tradition, this is what many minds are not prepared to admit. To them there is no distinction between saying that the narrative of a particular event in ancient history is, in its outward form, explicable by a reference to ancient modes of thought—no distinction between saying this and saying that the narrative is false, that it is a deliberate invention of the sort which we call a lie. This, again, is due to the fact of critical and historical studies being at the same time familiar to us and unfamiliar— the results of them known to many, the studies themselves altogether unknown to many more, who have yet a profound interest in some of their results. This is the difficulty of certain of us who are preachers of the gospel, yet not of the gospel as it was preached before the days of Copernicus, or Luther, or a later time—a difficulty which might almost remind one of those travelling merchants who solicit orders for their wares, not by producing their stock, but by showing certain patterns and some samples. Such is our difficulty that in consequence of it the question may arise here and there whether we really represent the old established firm from which we profess to come. Much of our preaching is a case of the samples being shown where a doubt is possible as to the existence of the stock.

If, in general, people who hear of certain results of critical and historical studies, and are staggered by them in some of their religious beliefs, were only familiar with these studies themselves, they could not but know as well as they know any fact of history, that no mistake could be greater than to ignore the distinction in regard to historical writings between deliberate falsehood and the shaping effect upon events and series of events of the thoughts and feelings of the particular age or place in which these writings appeared. But, as it is, this distinction being ignored in so many religious minds, what happens in the particular case with which we are concerned is, that the wonderful and miraculous connected with the most wonderful event in history has no significance, or next to none, for the majority of minds in our time. So far they are affected by one mode of thought, that of their own time, the influence of which they cannot altogether escape—that to which the wonderful requires to offer some explanation of itself. So far, also, they are affected by that other mode of thought belonging to an earlier time, which makes no distinction between history the details of which cannot be verified, and deliberate invention of the lying sort. And, thus confused, they make a response to the wonderful connected with the greatest event in history which, I think, is to be measured as regards religious emotion, by the fact that in the celebration of Christmas there is for the few rather than the many much remembrance of Christ, much of the jubilation of that multitude of the heavenly host to which the shepherds listened in the plains of Bethlehem.

In an age like this, of inquiry and criticism, it has often been said that earnest, real religious thought is to be looked for rather outside of the so-called religious world than inside it—the reason of that being that opposition to ancient modes of thought, where it exists, is thorough-going, earnest, single-minded; while assent to these same modes of thoughts, where it is given, is given only in a kind of a way, with reservations and qualifications which make of it more or less of an unreality. This is the meaning of that saying—

> " There is more truth in honest doubt,
> Believe me, than in half the creeds."

In that confused state of mind the confusion of which is due to the mixture of new with ancient modes of thought, it is possible for people to dispute nothing in the creeds and yet believe nothing in them. All that was once real in ancient beliefs may thus become to the modern mind a shadow of itself, a shade, or the shadow of a shade. It is so, I think, if not with regard to the supernatural as a whole, yet in regard to almost every particular instance of it which is noted in history. How far it is so can be measured, with some approach to accuracy in the particular instance we are considering now—the wonderful connected with the birth of Christ. Nothing was more real than all that to the thought of other ages. How far is it so to ours? I do not mean to ask, in saying this, what reasons we have found in our modern science and criticism for doubting it, which at an earlier time did not occur to the inquiring mind. The question is rather, Has not our whole mode of thought in modern times in regard to the wonderful, the miraculous, been so transformed that what we read of it now makes any impression of truth and reality upon our minds with difficulty, and only, if at all, by the help of other religious impressions and convictions of ours? It is not that we, at this distance of time from the heavenly host praising God by night in the plains of Bethlehem, have questions to ask which once would not have occurred to anybody as to the evidence for such a manifestation of the supernatural; it is that thought has travelled so far away from the point at which it stood eighteen centuries ago, and at which it was fixed for many centuries after, that now the impression which is made upon it by the wonderful event is comparatively feeble and uncertain. We cannot go back in thought to Bethlehem and see and hear with the eyes and ears of men to whom the visits of angels to this world were neither far nor few between. So, where there is not direct challenge or denial of the wonderful connected with the birth of Christ—as there is with regard to all that is supernatural—there is what is far more to be questioned, total unreality, belief without faith, assent without heart, thought without vision. So shadowy has the angelic host become to mortal men now, to whom in their direst need or in their loftiest ecstasies no angels come, that the joy of that angelic host over the birth of the Saviour of mankind, so far from communicating itself to the Christian world of to-day, as it did once, is never felt save at Christmas, and then it would be hard to say by whom.

This is not as it should be. To the thought of Christian men and women eighteen centuries

turies ago the angelic host and their joy were real. Why should they not be so to our thought too? That these men and women were even as we are, is the key to all history. That which explains the past to us is, above all, that which links it to the present—the certainty of all certainties the greatest, that, essentially, human nature and human life are in every age and every place the same. It is to recover the meaning of obsolete modes of thought when it has been lost to assume that thought is one, that the history of it is continuous and unbroken, and to go back with this idea over the ground it has travelled and note the conditions and circumstances by which its course has been shaped and determined. This is what has been done for a large number of minds to some extent in our time by those studies to which I have referred, by those critical, historical, scientific studies, the result of which is to show us the wide distinction there is between tradition coloured by the thought and feeling of an age and the work of impostors or knaves palming off fable upon the world as genuine history. True to fact or not, these studies enable us to see that the natural, inevitable outcome of the movement of Christianity in the generations immediately following that of Christ and his apostles was that the eager and enthusiastic life of Christian believers, in its conflict with a world lying in wickedness, foul and loathsome even in its most consecrated places, should revert to the beginning of a new era of peace on earth and good will among men and glory to God, to find satisfaction and expression for itself only in the thought of its being inaugurated with some celestial pomp and magnificence. There was no falsehood or fraud or wilful imposition in this. As the history of human thought from the commencement shows us, it was that which could not but be, other conditions of the human mind being what they were.' It does not matter to us whether the history is verified or not in which the angelic host appear. As far as our religious life goes we are concerned not with facts of history but with ideas, ideas to which belong emotions, feelings, aspirations, such as express themselves in the song of the angels. The idea which shaped the history is what we have to recover, the meaning of the history as merely historical having been so completely lost to us by the heavens and earth having waxed old and been folded up as a garment. That idea is not strange to our modern thought any more than to the thought of any past age—it is that the life of the Son of Mary is divine, that in that life of goodness, patience, nobleness, purity, love, self-sacrifice, all of the divine that can be grasped by the human soul in its loftiest reaches, all of the divine, too, that is required to create a new heaven and a new earth wherein dwelleth righteousness, is contained and comprehended. That idea had its own vividness given to it in the first century of the Christian era by the contact of the living with the dead—the living to whom that idea was life from the dead, the dead world, as far as eye could reach or thought travel, lying in hopeless disorder and decay. Our time, like that time, has its own peculiar emphasis and force to give to that idea. As the universe is expanded to thought, thought from its furthest reaches returns upon itself with the more ardour and certainty, to find that man's life consisteth not in the abundance of the things which he possesseth, but in love towards man and faith towards God, in his life being dominated by that idea which is that of the Christian religion, because it is that of the life of Christ.

With all, therefore, that there is in our modern modes of thought to make the supernatural seem to us in fact, however it may be in name, one and the same thing with the incredible or faintly believed—with all that there is of this in our modern modes of thought, that which is in them, too, of a powerful apprehension of the idea of Christ's life as the most signal manifestation of the divine, is enough, if it be only well and truly considered, to make the angelic host and their song of joy as real to us as ever they were to any generation of men—much more real, at any rate, than they have been to many in this generation. If I have any joy in the progress of mind, from which this idea is not excluded, but in which it gathers force, I love to think of it as it existed in the minds of Christians 1800 years ago, surrounding itself with the wonderful, mysterious, miraculous, of which the air was then full and by which every great event was heralded or accompanied. I can appreciate that. I am moved by it to more appreciation of the idea than I should have without it. Even as we are, these men were. I am reinforced in my convictions of the truth of Christ's idea as to the divine, in thinking how true, how real it was to generations of men following his, whose modes of thought in other respects were the opposite of mine. In this view of things, whatever may be the case with regard to the State, it is certainly true with regard to the Church, that it is easy to see which is the stupid party. It is the party whose policy is to stake the existence of the Christian religion upon opposing with effect to modern modes of thought those that are ancient—to create for us, so to speak, the heavens and the earth exactly as they were before in many revolutions of mind they had waxed old and were folded up and changed. For the effect of that policy is to make all Christian thought and belief more or less unreal.

In this view of things, on the other hand, in regard to the manifestation of the divine in Christ, it is easy to see that every life that is now lived in which there is truth, faith, love, nobleness, every sign which there is to show that the course of human life is not downward but upward, is so much human experience, the effect of which is to make real to us now the thought of distant ages—that thought according to which the divine was never so manifested in this world as in that life the memory of which is associated with Bethlehem of Judea.

I hasten to add a word in conclusion as to the teaching of religious truth to the young. All that I have said, I think, goes to show that the difficulty on this score which is felt by so many good and earnest people is not insuperable. Give to the young all the acquaintance that is possible for them with the modes of thought and of expression on religious subjects of past ages. Let them read the gospels. Take them back to the history of Israel in the Old Testament. As for the marvellous, the supernatural in all this let it produce what effect it may upon their minds. The modes of thought of their own time will determine for them what they are to think of it. Do not anticipate that result by cramming their minds with doctrines and dogmas. Eschew the Catechism, and to the topmost shelf promote the Confession of Faith. Let the education which you give them be such that in regard to religious questions and ideas, as with regard to everything else, the modes of thought of the best minds of their own age may be not unknown to them. Give them the modes of thought of the past, just as they were expressed then, to think of, and when they are able to think they will find in them the truth that was in them, and it will be true to them—all the more true and real perhaps for being mixed with what is doubtful or even incredible. So, for instance, to them, even more perhaps than to yourselves, it shall be unspeakably true in an age of science more advanced than ours, and of scientific repudiation of the miraculous more direct than ours, unspeakably true, that once on a sudden on this earth there was with the angel a multitude of the heavenly host praising God and saying, "Glory to God in the highest, on earth peace, good will to men."

XI.

THE LAST JUDGMENT.

"Inasmuch as ye have done it unto one of the least of these my brethren, ye have done it unto me."—Matt. xxv. 40.

THAT man's inhumanity to man is to be avenged and redressed in the ultimate triumph of the truth in regard to man's relation to the world and to God, is the creed of the philosopher and the hope of the Christian. Wider and clearer views of human life and human society than were possible when investigation of the laws of the one was prosecuted without attention to the laws of the other, are now familiar to us. It is still true that there are more things in heaven and earth than are dreamt of in our philosophy. But there are not so many of these things as there once were. We have reduced their number by some considerable discoveries. One thing, at any rate, has to be subtracted from their number, and that is the human race, human society as an organic whole every part of which is necessary and accountable to the remainder. That is dreamt of in our philosophy. Our reading, our legislation, our thinking, even our theology is pervaded now as never was the case before by the idea of human society being a great whole to the well-being of which the well-being of all its parts is essential, of which no one part, even the most insignificant, can suffer or go wrong without detriment to the rest.

Apart from the benevolent or religious sentiments in human nature, an enlightened selfishness comes here into play to check war and murder, to antiquate rapine and violence, to make robbery and confiscation figures of speech in use only among politicians out of office, in a word, as far as may be, to avenge, redress, abolish man's inhumanity to man.

But there is a still more powerful force at work in the same direction. Religion, even the religion of Christ, under the misconceptions to which it has been subject in common with all things human, has sent on earth not peace but a sword. As much murder has been done probably in the name of religion as from revenge or ambition or the cause which sent so many ships to Troy. But as this was not the beginning of the story of religion, at any rate of the religion of the Son of Man, so it is not the end. Live and learn is the lesson of experience in regard to divinity as in regard to other things, and it means living to learn humanity. So it happens now that the direction which was given to the religious sentiment many ages ago, and from which since then many causes have combined to make it swerve fearfully—the direction which was given to it by Christ himself, it is forced now more and more to take and to keep by the advancing intelligence of the race, that, namely, which identifies duty to God with duty to man, connects reverence for the Highest of all with pity for the meanest thing that lives, lends the force of a divine commandment to the deepest and most universal of our human instincts, fellow-feeling, benevolence. In reference to this incomparable force as in reference to enlightened selfishness, we see how the triumph of truth, of wider knowledge, of advancing intelligence as to man's relations to the world and to God, is an effectual check upon man's inhumanity to man. Human nature is Christian, however little human life may be so. Civilization is, if not orthodox, evangelical. History is a commentary upon that gospel in which the text as it stands is admitted to be the truth.

There would of course be neither hopes nor fears in regard to another life if in this life humanity fulfilled its own ideal. That final judgment of which in the language of parable Christ has something to say, would have no significance to our minds if it were not that, in the judgment of humanity itself, human life is not all that it ought to be or might be. In any other case we should hear of a last great assize as of something in which we had not much more at stake than we have in a sunset in the tropics or an eclipse above the pole. As it is, the judgment, painted by the Master's hands, is final. Those who are condemned in it, those who are acquitted in it, are acquitted and condemned on the score of their humanity or their lack of it. And this, as we have just seen, is simply to register man's final verdict with regard to himself.

It is to make the last judgment arbitrary, and therefore provisional, to assume with regard to it many things which have been assumed with regard to it; as for example, that, as an effect of it, a great part of the human race for their sins and for their ignorance, for their free thinking or their free living in this brief life, will be consigned to torture without any end or measure. This is to make it arbitrary enough. But, in as far as it goes upon the ground of humanity and inhumanity, it is final indeed. It is so, not simply because it is God's judgment upon man, but because it is man's judgment upon himself. It is so because he who comes under it to be condemned, is condemned in being what he is and as long as he continues to be what he is, though not a moment longer. He is not sent away into condemnation except in a figure of speech. Condemnation is actually where he is and where he cannot but be, unless he could be sent away from himself.

Man is made for society, and neither here nor hereafter can you conceive of him as having anything but an impoverished, despicable, odious, intolerable existence, apart from society. Thus constituted he is subject to law. The law of his being and well-being, rightly understood, is, as we have seen, that he should not live unto himself, still less in the practice of inhumanity, but that he should live for others, in the exercise of humane and generous sympathies. As far as human history can teach us anything, this law is eternal. To be always defending Christianity is to assail it in the house of its friends, and to do nothing to strengthen it against its enemies, if indeed Christianity properly so called has enemies. But some who attack Christianity confound that of Christ with that of Christians who would certainly, according to their principles, have concurred with the Jews in putting him to death. People who attack Christianity thus should be reminded sometimes of the final judgment, not that with regard to which they have been often enough warned, but this one of the Master's—should be asked to reflect how well it accords with the best and highest thought of an age as enlightened as our own. There is one form of Christianity which, even from the most advanced thinkers, ought to get some credit, and this is part of that Christianity — this last judgment, condemning only what is condemned, blessing only what is blessed, in the very nature of things, in the very nature of man. Given the idea of another life and of some sort of tribunal and some sort of assize before which, on entering that life, the good and the evil have to appear, and how vast a scope is opened up to the imagination there! Every mistake that in this earthly darkness has been committed in regard to the present life has been projected into that region, and in being projected has been magnified and its distortion distorted, so that sometimes the most unjust, inhuman, capricious tribunal that was ever constituted upon earth, in order to seem just and pure and humane, had only to compare itself with that on which the Eternally Good has been seated. Not to speak of other more horrible instances, what a judgment mediæval notions or even those of the nineteenth century itself, have made of this last one in the minds of people whose conception was or is that Adam's first transgression is sufficient justification for God consigning infants to hell if they have not been fortunate in having believing parents, or one believing parent—I am not sure whether the exception turns upon having one or having two. What a judgment, too, they make of this last one when they assign to everlasting punishment black men who have never seen a white man, for not believing what white men never told them about the white man's Saviour! Is it not, then, something on which we have a right to found a claim for respect for the Christianity of Christ himself, that in contrast with all that has been grossly, wildly, inhumanly imagined of a final judgment, his final one represents a state of mind than which nothing could be more perfectly sober, intelligent, just, observant of reality and truth?

It is man's judgment upon man which is embodied in the Christian representation of the final judgment. Therefore it is final. Those distinctions which it makes are everlasting, not to be altered or repealed without re-making man and re-making the world. That which in presence of the Eternal is decisive as to the well-being or ill-being of man, is humanity or inhumanity. Here and hereafter it is the same. In that sense, spiritual religion has for its last word as well as its first, peace, good will, compassion, sympathy, kindness, humanity.

Among imperfect men and very imperfect institutions, however, humanity, where it does exist and where there is no doubt of its making progress, is apt to be imperfect, one-sided. And that one-sidedness is, if not represented in the last word of even the most spiritual of religions, in an important respect not distinctly repudiated by it, at least in minds which cling rather to the letter than to the spirit of the gospels.

I may call the last judgment the last word of original, primitive, undebased Christianity. That last word, I say, is humanity. But, as the particular aspect in which it is here regarded is humanity evoked by and practised upon the sick and captive, the naked and destitute, Christians who are literalists rather than spiritualists, have found in it confirmation of the mistaken notion that humanity has to do with the alleviation or redress of suffering and wrong, rather than with the prevention of it. It is a fact which it is impossible to doubt, without doubting all the experience of all mankind, that comparatively little can be done to alleviate human misery in many of its worst forms, while it is just as certain that much can be done to prevent it in every form. But these are facts which are ignored in the thinking of many religious people, and in ignoring these facts they are not a little influenced by their habit of not distinguishing between the letter which killeth and the spirit which maketh alive.

If it is a good thing, the best of all things according to the first and last word of spiritual religion, to sympathize with, to soothe, to relieve the sufferings of our fellow-men, it requires no argument to prove that it is a still better thing to obviate these sufferings. It is obvious, for example, that a humane mind must have more satisfaction in thinking of the ravages of small-pox being prevented by vaccination than in thinking of small-pox patients attended by humane doctors and visited by benevolent Christian ladies. It is a great matter that, when typhoid fever and other diseases are epidemic, benevolence is epidemic too, and that the resources of compassion on which human misery can draw are seen to be practically inexhaustible. But if through the discovery of the theory of germs, the labours of scientific physicians were successful in indicating the way to prevent such diseases, that would be a still greater achievement in the view of a humane spirit. What is true of bodily suffering is true of all suffering, of all imperfection, and evil. Prevention is better than cure. As far as small-pox and its victims are concerned, vaccination is better than the best doctors, the best nurse, the best clergyman, the best district visitor, all in one. So it is in regard to our social conditions of a morbid sort. So it is in respect to our moral and spiritual enormities and plagues, all our tyrannous and epidemic ills. It is not a rule by which to judge individuals, but it is a rule, that the work of preventing suffering and evil is, in the view of humanity, better and greater than that of alleviating suffering and correcting evil.

It is in ignorance or contempt of this principle that a kind of judgment is exercised here below which is supposed to have some correspondence with the judgment of the Eternal. On the strength of some casual, highly hyperbolical expressions in the New Testament, we have sometimes heard of a claim on the part of "saints" to "judge the world." These expressions have been held to mean that they will somehow have a hand in judging at the last the miscellaneous crowd of their fellow-creatures outside of their own circle. If such a function were to be assigned to them, many of them would have to be educated for it. They could certainly not be trusted to judge the world upon Christian principles or upon any principles, if the thing were to be done now and here; and it is not to be supposed that they would be any more competent to exercise such judgment hereafter in view of what they call a state of everlasting rewards and everlasting punishments. This may be said particularly with reference to the principle of which I speak, that of humanity being best exercised in the way of preventing evil. I do not speak of all Christians or of the best Christians when I speak of the saints who hope to judge the world. But among those of whom I do speak, we find that their judgments of mankind are determined upon the principle, the opposite of the true one, that to take a hand in alleviating distress is better than to spend a life-time in preventing it, or (which is the same thing) in contributing to human happiness and well-being.

A minister who saves souls by preaching, or by prayer, a tract distributor whose movements are like the wind blowing where it listeth, and in proportion as they are uncertain are supposed to be spiritual and to be attended with spiritual results; a wealthy man who gives large sums or leaves large legacies to churches or charities; a missionary who plunges into heathen darkness as into a sea, to swim, if it may so be, to some unknown shore; above all, one of those men who, either it may be from much benevolence or from much egotism and vanity, have their names mentioned in connection with every society and every movement for the cure of our social, moral, religious ills—these are the men whom, if you were to entrust the judgment of the world to some of the saints, they would be sure to place beside themselves in the best positions at the right hand of the Judge. And I do not say that these are not good men, or that the work which they do is not good work. Some of them are among the best men alive, and of their work it is impossible to speak in terms of praise too warm or emphatic. But the mistake which is made is, that in comparison with such men— with men, that is to say, who may be spoken of in a general manner as doing something or doing all they can for the redress of ills that affect mankind— other men who are still more serviceable to humanity, are either ignored or receive very scant justice.

I hope and believe that it is not true that the saints are to judge the world here or hereafter, except in that sense in which I have spoken of the last judgment being not so much God's judgment upon man as man's judgment upon himself. But if there were to be any judging of men by men, sinners by saints, unbelievers by believers, the judges whom we have known after the flesh would have to be educated. They would have to learn that, in the view of a truly humane spirit, an enlightened and divinely inspired humanity, the greatest benefactors of the race and noblest servants of the Eternal have been workers and toilers, many of them or all but a few of them outside of those organizations and movements the object of which is merely to alleviate and minimize existing evils—men whose work and toil and endurance has borne no official, certainly no ecclesiastical stamp, and has had for its effect to contribute to human happiness and to prevent evil rather than to minister comfort to the sick and suffering.

It is an infinitesimal fraction, at the most, of human thought and energy that can be thrown into the business of redressing and moderating what is wrong in the social condition of mankind. What thought and energy are thrown into it encounter special difficulties in having to deal with the most complex and mysterious of all organisms, society. All but the small fraction of human energy and activity must be thrown into the struggle for existence, and for existence not as it is, but as it might be. Hence, as a general rule, it is those men who are concerned in giving to this struggle for existence its right direction who are on the largest scale and in the truest sense the benefactors of the race.

Assuming this to be the case, I shall, before I conclude, advert to two aspects in which it should be taken as a principle to guide our judgment of our fellow-men—

(1) In regard to great men;

(2) In regard to men not great but good.

(1) For aught that I know, I should not be surprised to be told that what is called the Land Question is not to be solved eventually without reference to the labours of a man who, if he were to come forward at a meeting of farmers or of politicians on that question, would likely be regarded with extreme curiosity. So completely foreign, I mean to say, to his line of research does that question seem to be, that for him to take part among practical men in the discussion of it would be a surprise to his countrymen. That man is the naturalist Charles Darwin. It concerns the well-being of a great many people in this country besides landlords and farmers that the best possible use should be made of the limited amount of soil we possess in these islands. This is a matter of the greatest consequence not only to agriculturists but to the toiling millions in towns and cities who live almost by bread alone, because meat is too dear for them to buy. Well, here is a man who in his capacity of naturalist has been for a long time a most devoted, laborious, conscientious observer of facts, and, as I believe, to the satisfaction of the scientific world. Among other things that he has accomplished in that capacity he has

recently demonstrated that soil fit for agriculture is to a large extent the production of the common earthworm. It is quite conceivable, indeed it is highly probable, that this will turn out to be a discovery of capital importance in regard to agriculture all over the world, and in regard to one of the most important questions of the day here. Should that be so it would be an instance everybody could understand and appreciate of the devotion of a great naturalist to his special studies having results of perhaps incalculable influence on the well-being of mankind. It could easily be shown that other investigations of the same man have contributed to that well-being. It would be no less easy to show that where no immediate benefit to mankind, at least as regards material comfort and happiness, could be traced to his profound and far-reaching discoveries, they have unquestionably served to enlarge the bounds of knowledge in various directions, to amplify the human mind, to strengthen and equip human intelligence for penetrating farther into the secrets of that universal order which is to thought peace and to life power. What this man has done in this way he has done by such pure, unselfish, beautiful devotion of his life to one pursuit as very few men of any country or any age have been found capable of showing. But, for all that, you will hear religious, or rather ecclesiastical, mobs or their leaders, howl and jeer and hoot at the mention of his name. They compare his work with that of some man known to them, unknown to fame, whose habit is perhaps to rise at meetings at which no dissent can be expressed and protest against the spread of infidelity, against Darwinism, against science, against light and truth and common-sense (of course under other names), and they say, what a contrast between the one man's work and the other man's work! And so indeed there is a contrast, only not that which they imagine, and not to the advantage of the fool who has said in his heart that there is no God but the fool's God. It costs your oratorical bigot very little trouble after all to raise his protest against infidelity, popery, Darwinism, science, common-sense. When he is accustomed to the humour of public meetings he can protest for an hour as easily, I suppose, as he can put on or take off his coat or enter a cab or accept a presentation of plate. On the other hand, to do his work the naturalist has to spurn delights and live laborious days; no eight hours' bill for him, or half-holiday on Saturday. He must devote to his pursuit time, thought, anxiety, often health and life, as hardly man in any profession or in any trade is obliged to sacrifice any of these things. On the other hand, as I have said with regard to one of them, the work of the one man is different from that of the other in this respect, that when it is done it is of lasting, perhaps incalculable advantage to society, while as respects the work of the other, what is alone certain is, that for all the good that ever comes of it or can possibly come of it, it might as well never be done at all. I might name along with Darwin another man who, as being amongst ourselves, ought to be better known to us as a great thinker and discoverer. Without naming him, I can speak of a man into whose life from his devotion to science there has been crowded the work of a score, of fifty, or a hundred ordinary lives. It would be ludicrous to compare the work of such a man either as respects quantity or quality, either in respect of its extent or of its value to mankind, with the work, say, of a faithful preacher of the gospel, who is faithful in the sense of delivering always much the same sermon from a variety of texts. Sir Walter Scott, as we know, with a grotesque and humorous vehemence was in the habit of disclaiming any intention to benefit mankind by any of his works. His sole object was to help to amuse his readers. In saying so he drew one character—his own— without any of that regard to nature and to life which is characteristic of his genius. Never was there a life into which a greater amount of hard work was crowded. Its effect has been, as the effect of few lives has been or ever will be, to help the world to get its work well done and its suffering well endured, by supplying it with amusement and recreation for idle and unhappy hours. In this sense, how many men are there whom we could name or ought to name beside the author of the Heart of Midlothian, as benefactors of mankind?

To achieve even second rate or third rate distincttion in literature now-a-days means at least more work and better work than would make the fortune and establish the fame of I don't know how many distinguished local philanthropists. As a rule, perhaps, that work is not better paid than shirt-making, or not nearly so well as boiler-making, yet those men who devote themselves to it may not unreasonably console themselves, as they are obliged often to console themselves, by reflecting that the contribution which they make to the welfare of society is incalculably valuable. I would not like, for my part, to affirm that a man whose life has just been published, Richard Cobden, did not by himself do more good to his country and to the world than all the so-called philanthropists of his time put together, though what he did was done, you might say, not so much in the way of ministering to human suffering as in promoting the general welfare by the rectification of public policy. It is remembered against him that he once said that there was more useful information in a single copy of the *Times* newspaper than in the whole of Thucydides. It is not forgotten, either, that he described the Ilyssus as he once saw it in the dry season, and had something to say of it in comparison with the Missouri and the Mississippi more agreeable to Transatlantic than to classical tastes. No one who reads his biography, however, would think it fair to judge him by these things even in regard to his views of culture in general or of classical pursuits in particular; and if there were anything in these things to forgive it might well be forgiven to a man who in demanding cheap bread for his countrymen was more perhaps than any man in England a visionary, or at least an enthusiast, in his acceptance of the truth that man shall not live by bread alone.

I have observed one thing in most biographies of great men such as these, and that is, that however little identified with expressly religious or humanitarian institutions and movements, they have been as a rule in a remarkable degree actuated, not by other or baser passions and impulses, but by the spirit of humanity, by the hope and the determination to be useful to their kind, to leave the world better than they found it, to contribute to human happiness, to advance and increase the material and mental welfare of their fellow-men. Rarely, if ever, do you find this spirit absent from such lives. It is almost inconceivable that such lives should be lived if it were absent from them. Seldom is greed of money a powerful motive in such lives. You may say that they are often actuated by ambition, by the love of fame, by mere intellectual irritability and curiosity. But behind all such motives, or mixed up with them, you will find a large humanity, a deep interest in and sympathy with the joys and the sorrows, the good fortunes and the bad fortunes of the common herd of mankind.

It is necessary to remember this in judging of great men. To judge such men, keeping this in mind, is an education for young and old, especially for the young. Keeping this in view, we are in a position to receive instruction in the art of living from the great masters of that art, from those who have lived to the best purpose for themselves and for the world. For, contrary to much popular judgment, it is not only or chiefly or in any but the most subordinate measure men who have distinguished themselves by the exercise of humanity in the relief of suffering—it is not such men only or chiefly who have been benefactors of their race. It has been and it is men the end and object or, at any rate, the result of whose labours and sacrifices has been to substitute in human life and human society, wealth for poverty, cheap bread for dear, good houses for pest houses, commerce for the trade of war, temperance for teetotalism and drunkenness, light for darkness, good for evil—to carry forward in one direction or another that improvement of human existence of which even yet we have seen only the rude beginnings.

(2) With regard to men not great but good, the same principle holds. Commonplace as well as great men are to be judged with reference to the way in which their life-work contributes or does not contribute to the well-being of their kind, not merely, or above all, as to whether they do or have the chance of doing works of mercy and compassion and kindness. David Livingstone was aware of this and was thinking of it when, after having been years in Africa, he declared, with reference to that continent, that more good was to be done by emigrants than by missionaries. The greatest literary man of our age, as we know, was proud of a father who was a mason, because he was certain that the houses which were built by the old man were without exception well built. His father, it is safe to infer, was much more an object of reverence and admiration to him on this account than he would have been

for imitating in hodden-grey the pulpit piety and philanthropy of a clergyman in broad-cloth. He was right. That man who, with a feeling of duty to man as duty to God, lives well his life as regards his daily work and his relations with his family, his neighbours, his friends—who if he has to build a house can be trusted as under the Great Taskmaster's eye to build it of good materials and to build it well, renders a service to humanity than which, as far as motive and intention and results go, none could be higher or better. It is a poor affair compared with this to have a layman's gift for clergyman's duty, to have a turn for prayer or for preaching, or even to be inspired by Christian liberality in that form in which the churches are clamorous for it, when they tell men with twenty-five shillings a week or less, that the more they give to congregational, missionary, sustentation funds, the more they will have to spend in the grocer's shop and to put in the savings' bank.

There are many whose work is obscure and ill rewarded who perform it as badly as they are allowed to do. But there are many more, who are more or less conscious in doing their daily work in the factory, in the fields, in mines, on board ships, in that dismal domestic drudgery or rather slavery, in which the wives of poor men and of rich men too are doomed to pass their lives—there are many more who in doing their work in these places and these circumstances are conscious that it is work which must be done by somebody, that it is useful, that it means comfort and happiness to a few or many, and who in that thought are nerved more or less to work so as to deserve their wages, and more and better than their wages, and who often, in fact, in rather doing so count not their lives dear to them, but for the sake of lives dear to them sacrifice their own.

To be just to them remember the last judgment. It is not so-called Christian work which is best or most necessary for the well-being of the race, it is the common work of common men, done, as it is being done, not indeed by all of them, but by very many of them. It is not one of us sleek and comfortable and well-paid agents of wealthy and powerful corporations calling themselves churches, who preach the gospel to the poor, or it may be to the rich, in any case at so much a quarter—it is not one of our number who is worthy of your reverence if you have any to spare. Reserve it for such an one as you sometimes see returning from his work in the fields, in the factory, in the mine, a son of toil prematurely aged by work, his back bent, his limbs stiffened and distorted—returning from his slavish toil to what would seem to you a wretched, but is to him a cheerful home, of which he is the light and happiness, and say as you meet him, Well done, good and faithful servant! Stop his work, and what could you do by your charity to replace it? Stop the work of men like him, and how long would your benevolent societies be able to ward off bankruptcy in trying to feed the hungry and to clothe the naked?

There is one remark—I have left myself only time to mention it—to which all this leads and which connects it with daily duty and with common life. In view of that judgment of human life by character, which is last of all, final, inevitable for all men in this world and the next, it is our duty to cultivate humanity, not a one-sided but an enlightened, intelligent, reasonable humanity. Churches in this respect, I may say, lag behind the age. Their humanity, in many cases or most, is all mercy and no judgment, no intelligence or right reason. Their judgment of men and things in regard to humanity, so much are they exclusively devoted merely to alleviation of existing ills—their judgment of men and things is mostly out of date, would have seemed good a century ago, cannot but seem unaccountable a hundred years hence.

Christian society in general has something to learn on this head. It is in one sense the golden age of philanthropy in which our lot is cast, at least as compared with any age previous to ours. There is a profusion of compassion. Thanks to the Christianity of the gospels, the schoolmaster is abroad in the shape of public opinion and conventional sentiment, teaching us to be humane towards criminals, lunatics, paupers, shipwrecked sailors and fishermen, distressed foreigners here and in their own countries and islands, and friendless children—towards, in short, all the sick and destitute and suffering portion of mankind. What qualifies our satisfaction, however, with regard to the exercise of humanity in this form, widely as it is exercised, is the reflection that it serves to annul for the larger part of Christian society, the obligation to exercise it in a form in which its exercise is just as essential or even more essential to the progress and wellbeing of the race. There are not many people perhaps—I do not believe there are many—who hope to make capital out of benevolence here or hereafter, who calculate upon securing property in heaven at the price of giving a cup of cold water to the thirsty, by a little kind attention to the wretched, in this world. I do not believe that humanity towards the sick and suffering is much exercised from any motives but the best and purest. But exercised thus it is felt, not by the few but by the many, to be a discharge in full of social claims and obligations. That is the worst of what is best in our social life, except where it is far more distinctly understood and remembered than it commonly is that prevention is better than cure, that to contribute to the well-being of society is better and greater than merely to take a hand in the relief of suffering. Except where this is better understood and remembered than it commonly is, nothing is more usual than to feel that to be compassionate is the whole duty of man. Hence there are people whose conscience does not trouble them as to whether some foolish or unjust or unnecessary war is not partly of their making, because, if occasion should arise, they would undoubtedly be prompt to succour the wounded and to pension the widows of the slain.

People give liberally to charitable institutions and charitable causes. They think they have done as much for their fellow-men as they can be expected to do. They do not think it needful to question themselves severely as to whether they are not lending their support to, and helping to maintain, social conditions and institutions and usages, class distinctions and privileges and monopolies, political injustice and abuse, by which the improvement and the welfare of human society is more hindered and obstructed than by anything else. You meet on the platform of benevolent institutions benevolent looking and actually benevolent men, and often the same men are to be met with on platforms on which things are declared to be essential to the safety and the welfare of society which are only necessary in reality to the ascendency, the noxious ascendency, of one class of the people. To merit the "well done, good and faithful servant," of the last judgment of all, we have to beware of a humanity which is thus one-sided. It is not less but more our duty to see that the part we play in daily work, duty, in social life, is that which is dictated by enlightened judgment as well as by the spirit of humanity—it is not less but if possible more our duty to see to this than it is after the example of so many dear to God and man to clothe the naked and feed the hungry and comfort the sick.

XII.

THE VALLEY OF THE SHADOW OF DEATH.

"Yea though I walk through the valley of the shadow of death."—
Psalm xxiii. 4.

IN giving a sort of objective reality to mental combinations the texture of which is feeling rather than understanding, in giving a local habitation and a name to the result of experiences in the variety of which imagination is required to perceive a certain unity, poets are among the greatest benefactors of the race. Their function, in doing this, is to gather to a focus whatever energies minds less gifted with imagination possess, and bring them, thus concentrated, to bear with effect upon what is to thought and feeling either beautiful and pleasing or sad and terrible. In that expression of an old Hebrew poet, "the valley of the shadow of death," there is an illustration of what I mean. It summons the soul to put forth whatever might or energy it has for the struggle with what is darkest and dreadest in human experience—all that has in it the least of the lightsomeness of life, most of the chill and darkness and mystery of death. It does so by giving a sort of objective reality, an existence, as it were, outside of the mind, to all the ideas and impressions, moods and feelings, of which the mind is capable in the line of an experience the gloomiest and most trying of all. One by one, and in detail, it is difficult or impossible to cope with these gloomy and foreboding thoughts—unbidden visitors of the soul that will not depart when they are commanded. When they are massed together, and to some extent externalized in "the valley of the shadow of death," it is as if the soul were equipped and armoured to match its powers against them. We are debtors, every one of us, to that old poet, whoever he was, who, in ransacking a teeming brain—teeming with images of idyllic peace and happiness and also with images of nameless dread and gloom—lighted upon the "valley of the shadow of death," as Bunyan afterwards lighted upon a "place where was a den," and gave to all that in human experience which before death is worse than death itself, a local habitation and a name.

Different forms of the religious sentiment have their different values in regard to the dismal experience thus happily named. None of them has actually the value which is theoretically assigned to it. I cannot tell how much was religion, how much was natural temperament, courage, cheeriness, in the confidence of that old psalmist to whom the valley of the shadow of death was nothing alarming. For aught I know, there may have been as much of the one as of the other. Natural temper and disposition count for much, usually for more than anything else, in the most trying moments of human life. Then the natural man is apt to part company with his costume of habits and customs, and to show himself as he was born, the bravest of the brave, or the weakest of the weak. It is not the most pious man in the regiment, I suppose, who is always the coolest in the forlorn hope. Impending bankruptcy, the loss of a law-suit, "the spurns that patient merit of the unworthy takes," threatened bereavement,—these convulse religious natures sometimes, as some natures that are not at heart religious are never shaken by disaster of any description. Some men, like John Wesley, are brave on land who are great cowards at sea; others, like some of Elizabeth's buccaneers, are timid in regard to the last adversity occurring in a hospital, but undaunted in regard to it if it threatens in a gale. Not according to differences of religious belief, but according to idiosyncrasies of disposition or accidental habits of mind, the valley of the shadow of death varies its character, in these instances, with the distance from shore and the height of the ocean wave.

As regards the last fact of all, which makes all human life a tragedy, we, who look forward to it not without a shudder, can scarcely but be conscious of a touch of envy on hearing of coolies in St. Helena and other parts of the earth lying down to die as peaceably as if it were to sleep. You can scarcely call the fatalism of the Turkish soldiery at Plevna by the name of religious sentiment, yet that apparently was as good a recipe for coolness in presence of accumulated horror and distress as any to be found in a book more sacred than the Koran. I have heard it said by one of the most eminent surgeons of the day that there are men and women with no nerves. His experience, singularly wide and varied, has shown him that what is a terrible ordeal for one person in the way of physical endurance, is a trifling incident between breakfast and dinner for another. Natural disposition, quality of nerve, in the physical and mental sense of the words, has much to do with calmness, courage, confidence in regard to all that is named in naming the valley of the shadow of death. Though religious people will hardly allow it to be so, so it is—that has often far more to do with heroism in its most striking forms than the religious sentiment.

But the religious sentiment *has* to do with it; and different forms of the religious sentiment have, or seem to have, different values in this respect. Those with which we are the most familiar are those, of course, which it is most worth while for us to compare and judge. If I go back upon ancient history, in obedience to that custom which we have of studying human life rather in a museum of antiquities than in nature, I cannot but be struck with the fact that it is rather among the Greeks and Romans than among the Hebrews that heroism, of the showy sort—heroism in presence of danger and calamity—finds its showiest and most manifold illustrations. Not to speak of Stoics and Epicureans among the Greeks and Romans, in whose modes of thought it is difficult to distinguish the precise influence of what we would call religious sentiment, there is in the history of these peoples, slight and poor and feeble as it seems to us their religious life was, heroism of this kind, in comparison with which all that is notable in the records of the Hebrew race, with all their religious earnestness and enlightenment, is hardly worth mention. Name Plutarch's men, and what a company they are in the matter of courage compared with the patriarchs, chiefs and kings, slingers, spearmen, and statesmen of your sacred books! Yet here, again, qualities of race, peculiarities of social and political condition, and, arising out of these or associated with these, natural temper and disposition in the case of exceptionally endowed and gifted individuals, claim to be taken into account. That it is glorious to die for one's country, was a sentiment which the whole life of the Greek and Roman fostered in a manner comparatively unknown to the wandering Arab who, as belonging to one of the twelve tribes of Israel, had found a home and dwelling place in the Land of Promise. That sentiment produced its natural effect in Plutarch's Lives—the reading of which is like reading the Charge of the Light Brigade. But it is when we come down to a later period in history than that in which there is either a Hebrew people or a Greek or Roman one, that we come upon heroism which is not that of the general and his staff, but that of the rank and file—heroism in which, in its own way, we have a deeper interest than in any recorded in history. Come down to Christian times, when you have the religious sentiment—the rise of which takes you back to the date of the 23rd Psalm, and beyond that date—so pervading the lives of multitudes of common men and women that their lives, on close inspection, are found to be instinct with a courage and endowed with a patience which can hardly be matched in Plutarch's Lives. That religious sentiment is what we have in the poem in which the valley of the shadow of death looms into view—one in which the soul has immediate perception of a Divine Helper, Protector, Shepherd, Friend, whose presence is an antidote to all alarm. What that sentiment has done to lighten, for countless multitudes of human beings, all adversity, and the last adversity of all, to make the unendurable tolerable or even welcome, may be partly imagined but cannot certainly be told. It has been that medicine for the sick and wounded and fainting heart which, at any rate, within the compass of our Western civilization, has done more for the relief of man's estate, and therefore for the glory of God, than all our panaceas put together—scientific discovery, progress in the arts, social, political, moral, spiritual reform and improvement. It is still what it has been—to multitudes it is still what nothing else is or could be in the way of solving the enigmas of life and making the heavy and the weary weight of it intelligible and supportable. There are worse ills than death itself. Exemption from the worst of them no man can achieve or purchase any more than exemption from death. If a man has a life to live at all, in his activities, in his emotions, in his sympathies, in his intellect, he is liable at every moment to disaster, from which death may seem to him to be the one relief to be thought of and prayed for. This is the valley of the shadow of death. Happy the man who, at such moments, like our old Hebrew poet, with our old Hebrew poet's song in his mind, can feel and does feel that neither is he quite alone and unsupported, nor is that Divine Friend, Helper, Shepherd, Succour, who is beside him, unable or unwilling to take care of him. Call no man happy till he is dead except this man who needs care so little how soon or how long he has to walk through the valley of the shadow of death.

All this can be said with truth. But yet it is not the whole truth. What truth there is in it must be taken with qualification and reserve. After all, it has to be admitted that courage in the last and worst extremities of human life is like those victories two of which have been said to be equivalent to a defeat. It is only making the best of what cannot be helped, bad enough in itself at the best. With regard to this life, to which all certainties belong, it can only at the best be reckoned a sort of drawn battle, when in the face of peril and the extremes of adversity the soul knows how to preserve something of its composure. There is more at stake in existence than just not to be thrust out of it with ignominy. It is, or ought to be, comparatively a small part of man's life, in which all his force is required to say, Never despair. It is, to be sure, only in the conflict against the heaviest odds that the soul recognises fully its own force. It is in such conflict that the powers of the soul, with all that belongs to their exercise, of a life, better and nobler than that of sense, are often brought to their highest pitch of vigour. How tame, after all, are the idyllic scenes of history and poetry compared with the tragical scenes of which history and life are full. If we had to choose between the one and the other in respect of quantity, we should say, without hesitation, perish a thousand of the idyllic rather than so much as one of the tragic—one, that is to say, in which there is exhibited the godlike force of the human spirit in its conflict with the worst and heaviest calamity and the direst need and danger. A good man struggling with adversity is a sight for the gods, and for whatever is godlike in us. It rouses us to a consciousness of ourselves, not altogether of the earth, earthy, as nothing else we see or imagine ever does. But, all the same, it cannot be considered the end and aim of existence, when the time comes for us to die, to do so with dignity. The larger part of life, if it is to be counted life at all, and not distinguished from death as simply worse than death, must be something in the way of activity, enterprise, enjoyment, rather than mere endurance however stubborn or heroic. If most of the life of man were naturally and necessarily to be passed in the valley of the shadow of death, it would be hardly worth while for the bravest to make any struggle for existence. The valiant would do well to follow the coward's example, and give up the conflict as soon as it begins.

This is one consideration which has to be taken into account to qualify the statement, that happy is the man who has learned something of heroism, or has in him something of it by nature. Connected with this consideration is another, which also has its weight. It is even less conceivable that thought should have stood still at the point which it had reached in any period of the history of Israel, than that the sun should have stood still upon Gibeon, and the moon in the valley of Ajalon, to witness a combat between the Israelites and their enemies. Thought has its progress to make, whatever else in the universe moves or stands still. The ocean is not so restless as thought, for the ocean sometimes slumbers—thought, never. And thus it happens that the religious sentiment has no forms fixed for all generations. It must accommodate itself to one form after another, to successive, sometimes almost opposite modes of thought. That form in which it prevailed among the Hebrews had its defects, if it had also its merits and advantages, and in inheriting it from them the Christian world inherited the defects as well as the merits. What of courage it imparted to the struggling soul, struggling against the direst odds—it obtained at the expense of the manner of thought with which it was associated and to which it belonged, being narrow in its scope, and, therefore, as regards life in general, unformed and unregulated. It did impart courage, as bringing the Eternal and Almighty, as the God of Abraham and Isaac and Jacob and every descendant of them, near to most hearts in Israel, near and friendly and helpful at certain moments. But it did that at the expense of Jewish thought remaining Jewish, that is, so contracted and distorted that, for us, Jewish life is very far indeed, even the best of it, from seeming ideal or divine.

We might wish to have the courage of some of the Hebrew singers and heroes, the courage which their ideas of God as their God, and of Providence as a scheme for the benefit of one people, gave them in trying moments. But except in as far as they were tutored by their national experience to love righteousness and hate iniquity, we do not desire to revert to the manners and customs, the ideas, the institutions, the social and moral and spiritual condition of the Hebrew race. In some of our modern modes of thought, God has receded to an infinite distance from us. So at least it might seem to us, on comparing some of our ideas of the universe with those of ancient times. When the question whether a personal God is thinkable is a question freely discussed; when a mechanical explanation of the universe has gone so far as to have its effect upon all minds in the way of shaking or setting finally aside all other explanations as partial and untrue; when in this mechanical explanation of the universe so little room is left for Creation, or Providence, or Redemption in the accepted sense of the words, it is certainly as if the Creator, Preserver, Redeemer, Friend of mankind, of more ancient modes of thought, had withdrawn Himself altogether beyond the reach of our importunity. That is what is felt with various degrees of concern and sadness by multitudes of men and women, in whom the religious sentiment is alive and active. "Heaven, even the heaven of heavens, cannot contain Thee," could be the thought of even a Hebrew sage in regard to the Maker of all. But then his heaven, even his heaven of heavens, was but a spacious tent stretched over a measurable sweep of sea and land compared with what baffles our imagination in the idea of infinite space. In the revelation which has been made to us by the telescope and the microscope, and, I may add, the spectroscope, of the infinitely great and the infinitely little, and of that unbroken chain which binds together every part and every movement of the great whole, from that darkness which is on the side of minuteness to that other darkness which is on the side of inconceivable remoteness—in the revelation which has been made to our minds of the heaven of heavens and of what it contains, it is as if God were not so much in retreat from us, but as if the last step had been taken and He were lost to thought. That old familiarity with Him in which there was no irreverence, born of the thought that His dwelling place was with the children of men or not far from them—that seems to us almost a lost sense of divinity in the universe. It was then as if men could speak to Him, and hear Him speak almost as friend conversing with friend. Out of the depths, the greatest to which descent was possible for them, they could cry to Him and be heard in the heights where He was. If direct intercourse with Him failed on occasion small or great, means could be used to establish communications with Him in which there was more or less of clearness and certainty. Thus, witchcraft and magic, alchemy, the appeal to the lot, definite answers to prayer, special providence, all had their day, and that a long one. Long after the middle of last century was past, Goethe's mother, inheriting along with other modes of thought some as ancient as the Psalms or the Pentateuch, could, with confidence in the result, prick her Bible with a pin to have it shown to her by a passage in the book what would be the issue of her son's illness. God receding farther and farther from man and his small world, as that world grows smaller in the account of the universe, and yet near enough to be within call, and by various means, if need were, to be brought nearer—it is this on which we look back on making a survey of the religious thought of many ages past. And in our new modes of thought, it is as if this chapter of history had been brought to a sudden close in the rise of a scientific no-knowledge, from the influence of which no creed and no Church can wholly deliver any soul of man.

So much is the religious sentiment obliged to be what modes of thought make it. But in submitting to this necessity the religious sentiment only seems to lose its value. Its value is not actually lessened by any change in our modes of thought which is in the direction of a wider and clearer comprehension of the whole of which we are a part. If it was an advantage, especially in the darkest hours of human experience, to have that familiar intercourse with the Maker and Preserver of All which ancient modes of thought gave to the struggling soul—if that was an advantage, there had to be set against it the imperfections and distortions of those modes of thought by which life in all its experiences became more or less darkened and confused. It was an advantage for a part of life, the darkest part, the smallest part, which was purchased at the cost of all the rest of life being darkened. So now, if in our modes of thought that advantage has been so far forfeited, the loss is compensated by what they are fitted to do for us in the way of ordering all our lives away from and not into the valley of the shadow of death, or the deepest part of it. You cannot have your Old Testament Shepherd-God exactly as the Hebrews had Him, without all their ideas of the world and life,—good, bad, and indifferent —being yours, and all your experience being fashioned as theirs was. If, on the other hand, for the idea of a Providence which is fitful and partial and erratic, there is given to you the idea of law and order in the whole universe, supreme, inflexible, eternal—if this is what you get from your modes of thought being what they are, you get from them a view of life, duty, destiny, in which there is more of order, less of confusion and darkness, than any which presented itself to the human mind in any past age. That is the great consideration to be taken into account in valuing the religious sentiment in this or that form. The form is determined by changes which are inevitable in the modes of thought of successive generations of men, and every form has all the advantages and disadvantages of that mode of thought by which it is determined. What is gained in one form is not lost in another, except in regard to a part, rather than the whole, of human life and human experience. The good man, the religious man of to-day, even in view of all that is darkest in the shady side of human life, is at no disadvantage as compared with any man like himself in his character, and unlike him only in his theological or scientific ideas. To be sure, we are sometimes tempted to envy those religious people, living in their ideas not in this century but in one remote from this, who, because they are almost as familiar with God as with their clergyman, have sometimes a singular fortitude and equanimity and patience in circumstances in which heart and flesh are apt to faint and fail —would fail but for the sense of divine support.

But then we have to think of what the ideas of most of these people are as to human life and destiny, their artificial piety put for natural, their sympathies restricted to an ecclesiastical denomination as the household of faith—their anticipations of a heaven for themselves which no generous or noble mind would be thankful to enter—their assurance of eternal torment for all mankind except that handful to be plucked as a brand from the burning. We have to remember at the same time, how everything, or almost everything, in their lives and the lives of others, stands, as they think it does, at the disposition of an arbitrary will. Their experience being that of hangers-on on a providence, the ways of which are dark and mysterious, not to say erratic, it cannot but be mostly of doubt and uncertainty as to all the issues of life except one—namely, that we must all die. We have to think of all this when we wish to estimate the value of the religious sentiment in the form in which it seems to bring God near at critical and desperate moments of human life. All this goes with any courage which is imparted by this sense of nearness to the Divine Being and familiarity with Him, and it cannot be detached or divorced from it. You cannot have the sentiment and not the thought.

On the other hand, in the larger world of

modern thought, if God is at a greater distance, or seems to be so, it is because that intervenes in which there is divine light and divine help for mortal men. "Whatsoever a man sows that shall he also reap;" all the universe, as we read it, is a witness to that, and a hieroglyph and picture of it. Be just and fear not. Be good, do good, and get good. The best that is in you to think and feel, *that* feel, and think, and do, and it shall be well with you, as well as the best that is in man to think, could think, or desire. Heaven there is none for the human soul, hell there is none for it, but in itself. The universe is the good man's friend and the bad man's enemy. It is as natural to die as to be born, and all the valley of the shadow of death, except what we make terrible for ourselves, by our misdeeds, is an illusion of the mind which clings rather to the shadows of life than to the great reality to which existence is more than life. All this is what, in the larger world, open to our thought, we read, mark, learn everywhere we turn our eyes—here one hint of it, there another, here one pictured presentation of it, there one more striking and elaborate. All this is that to which our modern modes of thought, all of them together, lend their force. The illumination in them is for the whole road on which we are travellers, not for a particularly shady league or two, or where it has been reported that Giant Despair has built his castle.

To make the best of life in the way of work, duty, pleasure, suffering, the last adversity of all, what could be better than that all this should be as real to us as it may be and ought to be. If this has any reality, certainty, indisputability, to a man's mind, he may say to himself, Can I by searching find out God? and yet add with a confidence which is no whistling to keep up his courage, "Yea, though I walk through the valley of the shadow of death I will fear no evil, for thou art with me, thy rod and thy staff they comfort me." It is enough to know of God that He is, and is the rewarder of those that diligently seek Him—if only in the sense that there is an order to which the idea of God is central, and according to which the good man and the bad man have a different life, and a different destiny, as different as heaven and hell. This is enough for the good man even in those hours of darkness beyond which there is no light, in which heart and flesh faint and fail—enough to give him a share of the experience of all who have lived indeed, for whom it was predestinated that death should have no sting and the grave no victory.

GLASGOW:
Printed at the University Press,
ROBERT MACLEHOSE, 153 WEST NILE STREET.

By the Same Author.

SALVATION HERE AND HEREAFTER:
Sermons and Essays. By JOHN SERVICE, D.D., late Minister of Inch. 4th Edition. Crown 8vo. 6s.

"We believe that never, since the literary splendour of the Scottish Church, in the middle of the last century, has it produced so many genuine fruits of learning and piety as at the present time. There are several names that might be cited, but we will confine ourselves to two volumes, those of Principal Tulloch and Mr. Service, which have lately appeared, and which in boldness of thought, and depth of insight into the real wants of the time, have not, we venture to say, been surpassed by any corresponding volumes that have appeared for the last ten years south of the Tweed. To those who think the Church of Scotland is bound up in a narrow Calvinism, it must be a surprise to find its chief pastors filled with a spirit which Jeremy Taylor would have honoured, and Schleiermacher would have welcomed, which Coleridge would have envied."—*The Times.*

"We have enjoyed to-day a rare pleasure, having just closed a volume of sermons which rings true mettle from title page to finis, and proves that a new and very powerful recruit has been added to that small band of ministers of the Gospel, who are not only abreast of the religious thought of their time, but have faith enough and courage enough to handle the questions which are the most critical, and stir men's minds most deeply, with frankness and thoroughness."—*Spectator.*

"Among the vast number of religious publications there are a few only which stand out prominently above the throng, attracting attention by any freshness of the expressions, originality in the thought, or by the clear light which they throw on obscure although familiar questions. Seeing that such volumes are scarce, it is the more needful that notice should be directed to them when they appear. A book which condenses much sound thinking in small bulk, and is manly in tone, liberal in sentiment, and full of healthy teaching."—*Scotsman.*

"There is no subject treated by Mr. Service in which we do not recognise a fresh and vigorous mind. He is always interesting. The volume is one which cannot fail to interest itself to all who seek to preserve amid the controversies and confusions of the time a faith to which they can cling, and by which they can live pure and manly lives. If the Church of Scotland can afford to keep such a preacher in such an obscure country parish, she must be richer in men and genius than any other denomination of Christians with which we happen to be acquainted."—*Glasgow Herald.*

"This is one of the few volumes of untheological discourses that is both readable and well worth reading."—*Church Review.*

"The world is always ready for a new prophet, and this time he turns up as the minister of Inch, in Scotland. He has the rare ability to think through the problems and questions of the day to their essential conditions and principles, and so plain and forcible are his words that you have to read these discourses a second and even a third time before you take in fully their wonderful inclusiveness of subject and incisiveness of thought. There is a vigorous and healthy religious life in these discourses, which will recommend them everywhere as the most important volume of sermons, for the variety of richness and reach of thought, which have appeared since the scanty reports of Frederick Robertson's discourses were given to the world."—*New York Times.*

MACMILLAN AND CO., LONDON.